APRENDA INGLÊS EM 30 HORAS

ALFRED BAUMGÄRTNER
e
ALEXANDER SCHÜSSLER

APRENDA INGLÊS EM 30 HORAS

REVISÃO DE: R. J. QUINAULT E H.-R. FISCHER

TRADUÇÃO DE: GUDRUN HAMROL

Editorial PRESENÇA

Todos os textos deste livro estão incluídos numa cassete.

FICHA TÉCNICA

Título original: *30 Stunden Englisch für Anfänger*
Autores: *Alfred Baumgärtner* e *Alexander Schüssler*
Revisão de: *R. J. Quinault* e *H.-R. Fischer*
© 1960, 1976 by Langenscheidt KG, Berlin und München
Tradução © Editorial Presença, Lisboa, 1993
Tradução de: *Gudrun Hamrol*
Capa: *Ponte da Torre de Londres (© Mauritius/Vidler)*
Fotocomposição: *Multitipo – Artes Gráficas, Lda.*
Impressão e acabamento: *Guide – Artes Gráficas, Lda.*
1.ª edição, Lisboa, 1993
Depósito Legal n.º 63354/93

Reservados todos os direitos
para a língua portuguesa à
EDITORIAL PRESENÇA
Rua Augusto Gil, 35-A   1000 LISBOA

Índice

Prefácio	9
Sobre a pronúncia inglesa	10
1. Meet John and Jane Brown	15
2. Getting Up in the Morning	19
3. Having Breakfast	23
4. On the Way to the City	27
5. Jane Starts Work	31
6. At the Post Office	37
7. Let's Have Lunch	41
8. Writing a Letter	47
9. The Browns' Home	52
10. An Evening at Home	56
11. At the Airport	60
12. A Walk in London	67
13. A Road Accident	73
14. Theatre and Cinema	78
15. Visiting the Houses of Parliament	84
16. Fleet Street and Its Newspapers	89
17. London Concert Halls	95
18. Sport in England	100
19. A Letter to Germany	104
20. Dining Out	109
21. The BBC Television Centre	114
22. Shopping in Town	120
23. In the East End	126
24. By Boat to Greenwich	132
25. Interesting Places around London	136
26. London Theatres	140
27. Goodbye to Karl	144
28. First Impressions of New York	149
29. A Bird's-eye View of New York	155
30. Conversation in a Drugstore	159
Chave dos Exercícios	165
Vocabulário	181
Índice de matérias	209

Prefácio

Uma longa experiência no campo do ensino de adultos levou-nos à presente reformulação deste Aprenda Inglês em 30 Horas. Foi nossa intenção criar um livro que possibilite uma rápida compreensão das características desta língua estrangeira.

Estas 30 horas de inglês são precedidas por uma introdução à pronúncia, para familiarizar as pessoas que utilizem o livro com as particularidades de sons ingleses.

Os textos oferecem uma perspectiva do quotidiano inglês. Apresentam a linguagem usual com que dominamos as situações do dia-a-dia. Dá--se ainda, em esquema, uma primeira impressão da cultura e tradição e ainda das instituições inglesas. As ilustrações facilitam o entendimento dos textos e clarificam os seus aspectos gramaticais.

A lista de palavras no fim do livro, constitui um auxiliar para uma melhor compreensão dos textos, por meio de transcrição em símbolos internacionais e da respectiva tradução.

A parte gramatical de cada lição está intimamente associada ao conteúdo dos textos, torna compreensíveis os aspectos linguísticos e parte dos exemplos para as regras. As tabelas e os modelos representam a matéria de modo claro e fácil de fixar.

O que se aprende é consolidado em exercícios cuja resolução pode ser verificada posteriormente, consultando a «Chave dos exercícios» (pág. 164 e seguintes).

Há ainda um índice pormenorizado de termos gramaticais.

Esperamos que este manual mereça um bom acolhimento por parte dos leitores.

OS AUTORES E EDITORES

Sobre a pronúncia inglesa

É difícil reduzir a pronúncia a regras. As mesmas letras ou os mesmos grupos de letras podem ter pronúncia muito diferente em palavras diversas. Por outro lado, o mesmo som pode ser representado por conjuntos de letras totalmente diferentes. Por isso, a transcrição fonética para cada palavra da lista vocabular e palavras das lições é muito importante, uma vez que não podemos deduzir com segurança a pronúncia de uma palavra a partir da sua grafia.
A seguir vamos explicar os símbolos desse alfabeto fonético. Além disso vamos descrever os sons típicos ingleses, isto é, os sons que diferem das vogais, ditongos e consoantes portugueses correspondentes. Esta transcrição fonética é sempre e apenas um auxílio. Não pode substituir o exemplo vivo, dado pelo professor, por um disco ou por uma fita magnética. Mas é importante para a tomada de consciência das diferenças essenciais entre os sons portugueses e ingleses.

1. Sinais gerais

O símbolo aparece sempre entre parêntesis rectos: English [ˈɪŋglɪʃ].
O acento precede a sílaba acentuada [ˈ]. Uma vogal longa é seguida pelo sinal [ː].

2. As vogais inglesas

[ɑː]	*a* aberto semelhante ao de «ah!»		
	car	[kɑː]	carro
	park	[pɑːk]	parque
	far	[fɑː]	longe
[æ]	som intermédio entre o nosso *a* fechado e *e* aberto (entre «da» e «pé»):		
	man	[mæn]	homem
	can	[kæn]	poder
	mass	[mæs]	massa
[ʌ]	som aberto, curto, formado entre a parte posterior e central da língua, como em «dá»:		
	cup	[kʌp]	chávena
	but	[bʌt]	mas
	come	[kʌm]	vir

[ə]	vogal neutra, breve, central, semifechada, semelhante ao *a* de «da»:

        a   [ə]   um, uma
        London   ['lʌndən]   Londres
        Peter   ['piːtə]   Pedro

[əː] vogal neutra longa; não existe em português:
        were   [wəː]   eras, éramos, eram
        sir   [səː]   senhor (quando nos dirigimos a alguém)
        work   [wəːk]   trabalho

[ɔ] *o* aberto e breve semelhante ao de «pó»:
        clock   [klɔk]   relógio
        box   [bɔks]   caixa
        not   [nɔt]   não

[ɔː] vogal longa semiaberta semelhante ao *o* de «tome»:
        door   [dɔː]   porta
        four   [fɔː]   quatro
        law   [lɔː]   lei

3. Os ditongos ingleses

Em todos os ditongos ingleses o primeiro som é mais fortemente pronunciado que o segundo.

[ei] semiaberto, como em «leite»
        late   [leit]   tarde
        name   [neim]   nome
        lane   [lein]   viela, vereda

[ai] som aberto como em «pai»:
        I   [ai]   eu
        my   [mai]   o meu, a minha, os meus, as minhas
        time   [taim]   tempo

[au] som aberto como em «pau»:
        house   [haus]   casa
        now   [nau]   agora
        loud   [laud]   em voz alta, sonoro

[iə] som semiaberto e semilongo como em «ia»:
        here   [hiə]   aqui
        dear   [diə]   querido, –a, –os, –as
        peer   [piə]   par, lorde, nobre

[ɛə] não muito aberto, o semilongo; só aparece antes de *r*; não tem semelhança em português; talvez como «éa»:
        square   [skwɛə]   praça
        hair   [hɛə]   cabelo
        air   [ɛə]   ar

[uə] semiaberto, semilongo, talvez como em «rua»:
        poor   [puə]   pobre
        sure   [ʃuə]   seguro, certo
        tour   [tuə]   passeio

[ɔi]	som aberto como em «rói».

boy [bɔi] rapaz
annoyed [əˈnɔid] aborrecido
royal [ˈrɔiəl] real

[əu]	começa com [ə] e continua como u; não tem semelhança em português:

go [gəu] ir
so [səu] assim
only [ˈəunli] só, apenas

4. As consoantes inglesas

[l]	a) antes de vogais é semelhante ao português como em «lá»

lie [lai] estar (deitado)
English [ˈiŋgliʃ] inglês

b) antes de consoante ou em posição final é mais sonoro como em «tal»:
hold [həuld] segurar
full [ful] cheio
double [ˈdʌbl] duplo

[r]	só se pronuncia antes de vogais, no início de uma sílaba; é pronunciado com a ponta da língua junto aos alvéolos dos incisivos superiores. Depois de vogal só se pronuncia como ligação com uma palavra seguinte começada por vogal:

garden [ˈgɑːdn] jardim
run [rʌn] correr
right [rait] certo, direito
There is [ðɛərˈiz] há

[ŋ]	como en ng, mas sem pronunciar abertamente o g:

long [lɔŋ] comprido
ring [riŋ] tocar (campainha)
slang [slæŋ] gíria

[v]	como v em «vale»:

very [ˈveri] muito
every [ˈevri] cada
wives [waivz] esposas

[w]	pronuncia-se *u* breve:

will [wil] quer
queen [kwiːn] rainha
water [ˈwɔːtə] água

[s]	sibilante surda como em «sede»:

glass [glɑːs] vidro, copo
summer [ˈsʌmə] Verão
sky [skai] céu

[z]	sibilante sonora como em «fase»:

zoo [zu] jardim zoológico
is [iz] é, está
rise [raiz] erguer-se

[ʃ]	sibilante surda como o ch em português; «chá»:

fish [fiʃ] peixe
shop [ʃɔp] loja
rich [ritʃ] rico, −a, −os, −as

[ʒ]	sibilante sonora como j em português; «já»:		
	measure	[ˈmeʒə]	medir
	joke	[dʒəuk]	anedota
	bridge	[bridʒ]	ponte
[θ]	som surdo formado com a língua na base dos incisivos superiores, tentando pronunciar um t:		
	thank	[θæŋk]	agradecer
	think	[θiŋk]	pensar
	tooth	[tuːθ]	dente
[ð]	som sonoro formado com a língua na base dos incisivos superiores, tentando pronunciar um d:		
	the	[ðə]	o, a, os, as
	father	[ˈfɑːðə]	pai
	breathe	[briːð]	respirar
*[h]	este símbolo representa uma aspiração no princípio da palavra:		
	he	[hiː]	ele
	house	[haus]	casa
	how	[hau]	como
	São muito poucos os casos em que o *h* não é aspirado:		
	hour	[ˈauə]	hora
	heir	[ɛə]	herdeiro
	honour	[ˈɔnə]	honra

5. A ligação

Em inglês as palavras são ligadas umas às outras na medida do possível, principalmente quando se encontram vogal e consoante:

This is a book. [ðis‿iz‿ə‿buk]   Isto é um livro.
We are in a room. [wi‿ɑːr‿in‿ə‿rum]   Estamos numa sala.

6. Frases para exercício da pronúncia inglesa

Leia as seguintes frases em voz alta, dando atenção aos sons que pretendemos praticar. De princípio fale tão nitidamente quanto possível e tente vencer a tendência para aproximar a pronúncia da do português.

1. Atenção à ligação:

a) John is a mechanic in a London garage.
   [ˈdʒɔn‿iz‿ə‿miˈkænik‿in‿ə‿ˈlʌndən ˈgærɑːʒ]
   O John é mecânico numa oficina de Londres.

b) He is a young man of twenty-four.
   [hiː‿iz‿ə‿ˈjʌŋˈmæn‿əv ˈtwentiˈfɔː]
   É um rapaz de vinte e quatro (anos).

2. Atenção aos sons [ɔ] e [ɔː]:

a) John took a long walk on the lawn.
   [ˈdʒɔn tuk‿ə‿ˈlɔŋ ˈwɔːk‿ɔn ðə‿ˈlɔːn]
   O John deu um longo passeio na relva.

b) It is only a short walk to the house.
   [it‿iz‿ˈəunli‿ə‿ˈʃɔːt ˈwɔːk tə‿ðə ˈhaus]
   É só um pequeno passeio até à casa.

---
* Os exemplos correspondentes a este símbolo foram concebidos pela tradutora.

3. Atenção aos sons [b], [d] e [g]:

a) This egg is good.
['ðis‿'eg‿iz 'gud]
Este ovo é bom.

b) Bob goes to bed.
['bɔb 'gəuz tə‿'bed]
O Bob vai para a cama.

c) John's work is difficult and hard.
['dʒɔnz 'wəːk‿iz 'difikəlt‿ənd 'hɑːd]
O trabalho do John é difícil e duro.

4. Atenção aos sons [l] e [r]:

a) John wrote many letters to a friend in Edinburgh.
['dʒɔn rəut 'meni‿'letəz tu‿ə‿'frend‿in‿'edinbərə]
O John escreveu muitas cartas a um amigo de Edimburgo.

b) For breakfast father likes fried eggs and tea with milk and sugar.
[fɔ‿'breakfəst 'fɑːðə‿laiks 'fraid‿'egz ənd‿'tiː‿wið 'milk‿ənd 'ʃugə]
Para o pequeno-almoço o pai gosta de ovos estrelados e chá com leite e açúcar.

5. Atenção aos sons [f], [v] e [w]:

a) Every morning John shaves carefully.
['evri‿mɔːniŋ 'dʒɔn 'ʃeivz 'kɛəfli]
Todas as manhãs o John faz cuidadosamente a barba.

b) He washes himself with water.
[hiː‿'wɔʃiz him'self wið 'wɔːtə]
Lava-se com água.

6. Atenção aos sons [s] e [z]:

a) In these offices there are several clerks.
[in 'ðiːz‿'ɔfisiz ðɛər‿ə‿'sevrəl 'klɑːks]
Nestes escritórios há vários empregados.

b) Two cups, two knives and two plates were on a table.
['tuː‿'kʌps 'tuː‿'naivz‿ən 'tuː‿pleits wər‿ɔn‿ə‿'teibl]
Numa mesa estavam duas chávenas, duas facas e dois pratos.

7. Atenção aos sons [ʃ] e [ʒ]:

a) He had some fish for lunch.
[hiː‿hæd səm 'fiʃ fə‿lʌntʃ]
Ele comeu peixe ao almoço.

b) He had some money changed in a shop near his garage.
[hiː‿hæd səm‿'mʌni‿'tʃeindʒd‿in‿ə‿'ʃɔp niə hiz 'gærɑːʒ]
Ele trocou dinheiro numa loja ao pé da oficina.

8. Atenção aos sons [θ] e [ð]:

a) This is a tooth, these are my teeth.
['ðis‿iz‿ə‿'tuːθ 'ðiːz‿ɑː‿mai‿'tiːθ]
Isto é um dente, estes são os meus dentes.

b) Father cleans his teeth with a toothbrush.
['fɑːðə‿kliːnz hiz 'tiːθ wið‿ə‿'tuːθbrʌʃ]
O pai lava os dentes com uma escova (de dentes).

c) I thought you were thirsty.
[ai‿'θɔːt juː‿wə‿'θəːsti]
Eu pensei que estavas com sede.

Meet John and Jane Brown

Texto   **1 A**

This is John Brown and this is his sister, Jane Brown. They Live with their father and mother in a house at Wood Green, a suburb of London, and they each have a room upstairs in the house.

John is a mechanic and works at a big London garage. Jane is a secretary and works at an office in the City, the office of Johnson and Howard. The office is in Coleman Street.

John is twenty-four. He has a car of his own and drives to his work. Jane is twenty-six. She takes the underground to get to her office. The journey takes half an hour.

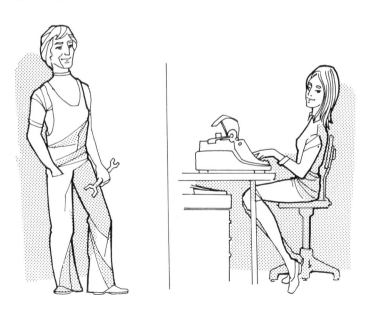

Notas gramaticais **1 B**

1. O artigo

> Jane is **a** secretary and works at an office in the City

O ARTIGO INDEFINIDO tem a mesma forma para os dois géneros (masculino e feminino): **a** [ə] (um, uma). Antes de palavras cuja pronúncia comece por vogal tem a forma **an** [ən].

> **The** [ðə] journey takes half an hour.
> **The** [ði] office is in Coleman Street.

O ARTIGO DEFINIDO tem a mesma forma para os dois géneros, no singular e no plural: **the** (o, a, os, as).
Antes de palavras cuja *pronúncia* comece por consoante tem o som [ðə].
Antes de palavras cuja *pronúncia* comece por vogal tem o som [ði].

2. O pronome pessoal

> **She** is a secretary.

São os seguintes os pronomes pessoais:

Singular		*Plural*	
I [ai]	eu	**we** [wi(:)]	nós
you [ju(:)]	tu, você	**you** [ju(:)]	vós, vocês
he [hi(:)]	ele	**they** [ðei]	eles, elas
she [ʃi(:)]	ela		
it [it]	ele, ela (neutro)		

3. O verbo

> John work**s**. [s]   He drive**s**. [z]

No PRESENTE (*Present Tense* ['preznt tens]) o verbo toma –s na 3.ª pessoa do singular (ele, ela; ele ou ela [neutro]).

Esse **s** pronuncia-se do seguinte modo:
  depois de sons surdos ([p, t, k, f, θ]) [s],
  depois de sons sonoros ([b, d, g, v, ð, m, n, l, r] e vogais [z]

I work	eu trabalho	we work	nós trabalhamos
you	tu trabalhas, você trabalha	you	vós trabalhais, vocês trabalham
he works **she** **it**	ele trabalha ela trabalha ele, ela trabalha (neutro)	**they**	eles, elas trabalham

As outras formas do presente não tomam qualquer terminação.

> **to work** trabalhar – **to drive** guiar, andar de automóvel

O INFINITO é precedido por **to**.

4. O presente de «to be» e «to have»

> John **is** a mechanic. He **has** a car.

As palavras *is* e *has* são formas de *to be* (ser, estar) e de *to have* (ter).

As **formas do Presente** de **to be** e **to have** são:

I	am [æm, əm]	eu sou, estou	I	have [hæv, həv]	eu tenho
you	**are** [ɑ(ː)]	tu és, estás você é, está	**you**		tu tens você tem
he **she** **it**	**is** [iz]	ele é, está ela é, está ele, ela é, está (neutro)	**he** **she** **it**	**has** [hæz, həz]	ele tem ela tem ele, ela tem (neutro)
we **you** **they**	**are** [ɑ(ː)]	nós somos, estamos vós sois, estais vocês são, estão eles, elas são, estão	**we** **you** **they**	**have** [hæv, həv]	nós temos vós tendes vocês têm eles, elas têm

5. O determinante possessivo

> He drives to **his** work.

Os determinantes possessivos são:

my [mai]	o meu, a minha, os meus, as minhas
your [jə(ː)]	o teu, a tua, os teus, as tuas
	o seu, a sua, os seus, as suas (de você)
his [hiz]	o seu, a sua, os seus, as suas (dele)
her [hə(ː)]	o seu, a sua, os seus, as suas (dela)
its [its]	o seu, a sua, os seus, as suas (dele, dela [neutro])
our ['auə]	o nosso, a nossa, os nossos, as nossas
your [jɔ(ː)]	o vosso, a vossa, os vossos, as vossas (de vocês)
their [ðɛə]	o seu, a sua, os seus, as suas (deles, delas)

> **my** father
> **my** mother
> **my** house
> **my** work

A forma do determinante possessivo é a mesma para os dois géneros e também para o plural.

Exercícios **1 C**

1. *a*) Empregue o artigo indefinido (*a* ou *an*) antes dos seguintes substantivos: sister, father, mother, house, suburb, room, mechanic, garage, secretary, office, car, underground, journey, hour.
   Lembre-se de que é a pronúncia do substantivo que conta e não a forma escrita.
   b) Substitua o artigo indefinido pelo definido (*the*). Lembre-se das diferenças de pronúncia deste último.
2. Complete as seguintes séries:
   a) I am a mechanic. *b*) I have a car.
   You... You...
   (Aqui forme apenas o singular).
   c) I live in London *d*) I am in my house.
   You... You...
   e) I drive to my office.
   You...
3. Transponha o texto para a 1.ª pessoa. Comece assim:
   I am John Brown and this is my sister, Jane Brown. We...
4. Preencha os espaços:
   John Brown ___ a mechanic. He ___ a sister. He works ___ a garage. Jane works at ___ office. John ___ a car. Jane ___ the underground. The journey takes half ___ hour. They each ___ a room in the house.

Getting Up in the Morning

Texto **2 A**

This morning John wakes up late, so he must hurry. He rushes into the bathroom on the other side of the landing and turns on the taps to fill the basin. In the meantime he shaves himself with an electric razor. Then he washes himself with soap and water, and cleans his teeth with a toothbrush and toothpaste.

Next he dresses himself and starts to comb his hair. But the comb breaks, so he takes one of his father's. His hair is too long: he must soon go to the hairdresser's. After combing his hair John hurries downstairs to breakfast.

Notas gramaticais **2 B**

1. O verbo

> I wash – he wash**es** ['wɔʃiz]
> I dress – he dress**es** ['dresiz]

Depois de sons sibilantes ([s, z, (t)ʃ, d(ʒ), ks]), junta-se **-es** [-iz] à 3.ª pessoa do singular.

> i hurr**y** – he hurr**ies**
> **mas:** I pla**y** – he pla**ys**
> (eu brinco – ele brinca)

Numa palavra terminada em **-y** este passa a **-ie** se for precedido de consoante. Se for precedido de vogal mantém-se.

2. Formação do plural

a tap	– tap**s** [tæps]
a journey	– jorney**s** ['dʒɜːniz]
a comb	– comb**s** [kəumz]
a brush	– brush**es** ['brʌʃiz] (uma escova – escovas)

Forma-se o plural acrescentando -**s** à forma do singular.
Depois de sons sibilantes acrescenta-se -**es** (-iz).
Para a pronúncia e escrita seguem-se as mesmas regras apresentadas para a 3.ª pessoa do singular do Presente (vd. 1B3 e 2B1).

3. O caso possessivo

a) **John's** parents live at Wood Green
b) The office **of Johnson and Howard** is in the City.

Para exprimir posse junta-se **'s** ao substantivo ou emprega-se a preposição **of**.

4. Forma e emprego do caso possessivo

John's room is upstairs.
His **parents'** house is in London
The room is on the other side **of the landing.**

1. Se o substantivo estiver no singular junta-se **'s**;
   Se o substantivo estiver no plural junta-se apenas **'** (apóstrofo).
   Para a pronúncia do **'s** seguem-se as regras apresentadas para a 3.ª pessoa do singular do Presente de um verbo (vd. 1B3 e 2B1).

2. Também se pode empregar a preposição **of**: **of the landing**.

> *a)* John takes his **father's** comb.
> *b)* **John's** work is in the garage.
> *c)* He must go to the **hairdresser's** (shop).
> *d)* He takes a comb **of his father's** (combs).

Emprego do caso possessivo com 's:
a) para exprimir a posse (o pente que pertence ao pai);
b) para exprimir o agente (o trabalho que John realiza);
c) para exprimir o local, que em geral se omite, por ex. to the hairdresser's (shop) = ao cabeleireiro; *at the Brown's (house)* = em casa dos Browns;
d) se a palavra que exprime o possuído (*comb*) for precedida por um artigo indefinido, por um determinante ou por um numeral, o substantivo que se segue a *of* tem ainda *'s*.

> The side **of the landing**.
> A suburb **of London**.

O emprego de **of** também exprime a parte de um todo.

5. O complemento indirecto

> Father gives **John** a comb.
> Father gives a comb **to John**.

O complemento indirecto pode empregar-se:
a) sem preposição, precedendo o directo;
b) a seguir ao directo, com a preposição *to*.

Exercícios 2 C

1. *a)* Forme o plural de: car, city, comb, garage, house, journey, landing, mother, office, razor, room, secretary, side, suburb, tap, toothbrush.
   b) Leia o plural em voz alta, tendo em atenção a pronúncia da terminação.

2. Traduza: o quarto do John; o outro lado do quarto; a casa do meu pai; os quartos da casa; a casa dos meus pais; a mãe acorda a Jane; a Jane dá a pasta de dentes ao John; o pai dá a máquina de barbear ao John e não à Jane; nós vamos ao cabeleireiro; eles estão em casa dos Browns.
3. Substitua o determinante possessivo pela palavra indicada entre parêntesis: his room (John); her office (Jane); their house (the Browns); their bathroom (the parents); its teeth (the comb); his shop (the hairdresser); its side (the landing).

Having Breakfast

Texto **3 A**

John comes into the dining-room. It is nearly eight o'clock. His parents and Jane are already having breakfast.

«Good morning», John says, and sits down at the breakfast table. In front of him there is an empty teacup. «Whose cup is this? Is it mine?», he asks.

«Yes, that's yours», his mother answers.

John helps himself to tea with milk and sugar; he prefers tea to coffee.

«What will you have to eat?» his mother asks him.

«Just cornflakes and toast, please. I must hurry.»

John's father likes a big breakfast, so he has some bacon and eggs first and then some toast with butter and marmalade. Jane just has some grapefruit, a cup of coffee and a slice of toast. She doesn't like to eat much breakfast.

«Another cup of tea?» Mother asks John. He looks at his watch. «No, thank you», he answers. «I really must go now. Goodbye.»

He takes his raincoat and hurries out.

«I must go too», says Jane.

Notas gramaticais 3 B

1. O pronome pessoal complemento

> Mother asks **him**.

A palavra *him* é o complemento directo da frase; é um pronome pessoal complemento.

Sujeito	Complemento directo ou indirecto	
I	**me** [mi(ː)]	me, mim
you	**you**	te, ti; o, lhe (você)
he	**him** [him]	o, lhe
she	**her** [hə(ː)]	a, lhe
it	**it**	o, a, lhe
we	**us** [ʌs]	nos
you	**you**	vos; os, as, lhes (vocês)
they	**them** [ðəm, ðem]	os, as, lhes

Quando complemento indirecto, o pronome precede o complemento directo.

2. O pronome possessivo

> Is this **my** cup? – No, it is **mine**.

Em 1B5 tratámos dos determinantes possessivos. A par desses existem os pronomes possessivos que não acompanham o substantivo.

my – **mine** [main]	o meu, a minha, os meus as minhas
your – **yours** [jɔːz]	o teu, a tua, os teus, as tuas
	o seu, a sua, os seus, as suas (de você)
his – **his** [hiz]	o seu, a sua, os seus, as suas (dele)
her – **hers** [həːz]	o seu, a sua, os seus, as suas (dela)
its – **its** [its]	o seu, a sua, os seus, as suas (dele, dela, neutro)
our – **ours** ['auəz]	o nosso, a nossa, os nossos, as nossas
your – **yours** [jɔːz]	o vosso, a vossa, os vossos, as vossas (de vocês)
their – **theirs** [ðɛəz]	o seu, a sua, os seus, as suas (deles, delas)

3. O pronome reflexo

> He helps **himself** to a cup of tea.

Himself é um pronome reflexo. Significa que o sujeito e o complemento directo são a mesma pessoa. **Ele** serve-se (a si mesmo) de uma chávena de chá.

Os pronomes reflexos são:

myself [mai'self]	me
yourself [jɔː'self]	te, se (você)
himself [him'self]	se
herself [həː'self]	se
itself [it'self]	se (neutro)
ourselves ['auə'selvz]	nos
yourselves [jɔː'selvz]	vos, se (vocês)
themselves [ðem'selvz]	se

4. O género dos substantivos

> John is a mechanic. He is a mechanic.
> Jane is his sister. She is his sister.
> He looks at **his watch**. He looks at **it**.

Para **pessoas do sexo masculino** usa-se o pronome **he**,
para **pessoas do sexo feminino** usa-se o pronome **she**,
para **coisas e abstractos** usa-se o pronome **it**.
Não são aqui consideradas algumas excepções a esta regra.

5. Emprego das preposições

> John sits down **at** the breakfast table.
> He has some tea **with** milk and sugar.
> He rushes **into** the bathroom.

At, *with* e *into* são preposições.
Nas lições 10-29 iremos continuar com este assunto.

Exercícios 3 C

1. Complete as seguintes séries:
   a) Mother gives me a cup of tea.
       Mother gives you...
   b) Jane asks me to help her.
       Jane asks you...
   c) This is my cup. It is mine.
       This is your...
   d) I help/wash/dress myself.
       You help... He...
       You wash...
       You dress...

2. Nas seguintes frases, substitua por pronomes as palavras em itálico:
   John Brow lives in *his parents'* house. *John* goes into the dining-room. *His parents and Jane* are already having breakfast. In front of *John* there are two teacups. In front of *Jane* there is a cup of coffee. Jane likes *coffee*. John asks *his mother* for some more toast. *Mother's* toast is always good. John takes *the cornflakes*. Is this *John's* cup? No, it is *Jane's*. Father eats two eggs; he likes *eggs*. Mother gives *Father and John* some marmalade. John looks at *his watch*.

On the Way to the City

Texto **4 A**

Wood Green Underground Station is only five minutes' walk from the Browns' house. When Jane reaches the station, she finds her friend Helen standing at the newspaper kiosk reading a paper.
«Hello, Helen, how are you?»
«Hello, Jane, I'm fine, thanks.»
«Wich paper is that, Helen?»
«The Daily Mirror.»
«I want to get the Daily Express today. It has an interesting article about the tennis championship in it.»
«All right, but hurry. Our train is coming.»
Jane gets the paper and they both go down to the platform.

The train arrives.
«Which carriage?» Jane asks.
«The front one, I think. It's not so full.»
They get into the carriage.

«Who won the tennis championship?» Helen asks.
«The American girl?»
«No, the Australian girl this time. She's very good.»
While the two friends are talking about tennis the train reaches King's Cross and Helen gets out. Jane opens her paper and begins to read. She has another five stations to go, which leaves her just time to glance through the article and the news.

Notas gramaticais   **4 B**

1. Os pronomes interrogativos

> **Who** is standing at the kiosk? – **Helen** is standing there.
> **What** is Helen reading? – She is reading **a newspaper**.
> **Which** carriage do [du] they take? – **The front one**.

Existem três pronomes interrogativos:
who? que se refere a pessoas (quem?)
what? que se refere a coisas (o quê?, que?)
which? que faz selecção entre um número limitado de pessoas ou coisas (que, qual?, quais?)

2. Formas do pronome interrogativo

Who won the championship?	quem?
Whose cup is this?	de quem?
Who is John speaking **of**?	de quem?
Who does Mother give a cup of tea **to**?	a quem?
Who does Jane see at the kiosk?	quem?

Nestes exemplos o pronome *who?* aparece com a forma *whose?* (de quem?), (exprimindo posse), a par de *who...of?* (de quem?), *who...to?* (a quem?).
Em linguagem culta existe a forma *whom?* que se emprega como complemento directo ou precedido de preposição (*of*, *to*, etc.).

3. What e which como determinantes

> **What** is Helen reading?
> **What** paper is she reading?
> **What an** interesting article!

No primeiro exemplo **what?** emprega-se como pronome.
No segundo exemplo **what?** emprega-se como determinante (junto de um substantivo).
What a(n)... é exclamativo (que artigo interessante!)

> **Which** of the two houses is yours?
> **Which** house is yours?

No primeiro exemplo **which?** emprega-se como pronome.
No segundo exemplo **which?** emprega-se como determinante.

4. Advérbios interrogativos

> **How** are you?
> **Where** is Helen standing?
> **When** does Jane read her paper?
> **Why** must the two friends go downstairs?

Os advérbios interrogativos indagam em que circunstâncias alguma coisa se passa:

how? [hau] = como? – o modo
where? [wɛə] = onde? – o lugar
when? [wɛn] = quando? – o tempo
why? [wai] = porquê? – a causa

5. Os pronomes relativos

> Jane, **who** works in the City, lives in a suburb.
> The paper **which** Helen has is the Daily Express.
> The Daily Express is the paper **that** Jane wants.

São três os pronomes relativos: **who**, **which** e **that** [ðət]. Os três correspondem ao português «que», «o qual», «os quais», «as quais».

Who refere-se a pessoas, **which** a coisas e **that** a pessoas e coisas. (Sobre o emprego de **that** vd. 22B6.)
Who e **which** tomam as formas indicadas para os pronomes interrogativos. **That** tem esta forma única.

6. Pronomes e determinantes demonstrativos

> **This** is Jane, **that** is John.
> **These** articles are interesting, **those** are not.

This [ðis] (este, esta) refere-se àquilo que está próximo, **that** [ðæt] (aquele, aquela) ao que está afastado.
O plural de *this* é **these** [ðiːz].
O plural de *that* é **those** [ðəuz].

Exercícios 4 C

1. Empregue os interrogativos adequados às seguintes perguntas (a palavra entre parêntesis no fim de algumas é indicativa do que se pretende).
   – is a young woman of twenty-six? (Jane)
   – is her office? (City)
   – is Wood Green? (subúrbio de Londres)
   – has a car of his own?
   – is John's room?
   – is the bathroom?
   – is already having breakfast?
   – is on the table?
   – cup is this?
   – office is in the City?
   – is standing at the newspaper kiosk?
   – is Helen reading?
   – paper is she reading?
   – is Helen?

2. Ligue as seguintes frases com um pronome relativo:
   Exemplo: Jane Brown is twenty-six.
              + She is a secretary in an office.
              = Jane Brown, who is twenty-six, is a secretary in an office.
   Jane works with Johnson and Howard. – Johnson and Howard's office is in Coleman Street.
   Jane lives at Wood Green. – Wood Green is a suburb of London.
   Jane has a brother. – His name is John.
   He rushes into the bathroom. – It is on the other side of the landing.
   He takes a comb. – It is one of his father's.
   John comes into the dining-room. – It is downstairs.
   Father likes a big breakfast. – He has bacon and eggs.
   Helen is standing at the newspaper kiosk. – She is reading her paper.
   Jane buys the Daily Express. – It has an interesting article in it.
   Jane opens her paper. – She has another five stations to go.

Jane Starts Work

Texto **5 A**

It is half past nine when Jane arrives at Bank Station and gets off the underground train. As she is later than yesterday, she hurries down Princes Street. It is full of office-workers going to their offices. The streets of the City are crowded now. In the evening they are almost deserted. There are not so many people then as during the rush hours.

Jane passes the Stock Exchange, the Mansion House and the Bank of England, three of the finest and most famous buildings in the City. Then she takes the next street to the left, which is the nearest to her office.

When she gets into the office, her boss, Mr. Holdstock, is already sitting at his desk.

«Good morning», Jane says. «I'm sorry I'm a little late.» «Never mind», he replies. Jane likes Mr. Holdstock. He is as kind as he is polite to her.

There are many letters on Jane's desk, some from Liverpool, Manchester and Edinburgh, and also some from France and Germany. Jane opens the letters and gives them to Mr. Holdstock. She uncovers her typewriter. She is very careful, more careful than she was a few years ago, when she was still a junior typist. She likes her work, and thinks it most interesting.

Mr. Holdstock, who speaks French and German and understands Spanish, is concerned with the foreign trade of his firm. He must know the current share prices, which he finds in the Financial Times. He always has the latest edition in front of him.

Notas gramaticais   **5 B**

1. Os graus dos adjectivos

> Father gets up **late**, Jane is **later**, John is (the) **latest** of them all

Nesta frase apresentam-se os graus do adjectivo **late.**

O grau normal, comparativo e superlativo são respectivamente *late* tarde – *later* mais tarde – *latest* o mais tarde.

Em inglês há dois processos para formar os graus: com as terminações **-er, -est** ou fazendo-os preceder de **more** e **most**.

2. Os graus formados com «-er», «-est»

a) short,	shorter,	shortest	
b) polite,	politer,	politest	
c) happy	happier	happiest	(feliz)
['hæpi]	['hæpiə]	['hæpiist]	
noble	nobler	noblest	(nobre, distinto)
['nəubl]	['nəublə]	['nəublist]	
clever	cleverer	cleverest	(inteligente)
['klevə]	['klevərə]	['klevərist]	
narrow	narrower	narrowest	(estreito)
['nærəu]	['nærəuə]	['nærəuist]	
handsome	handsomer	handsomest	(belo)
['hænsəm]	['hænsəmə]	['hænsəmist]	

Formam-se deste modo:
a) adjectivos monossilábicos,
b) adjectivos dissilábicos acentuados na 2.ª sílaba,
c) adjectivos dissilábicos terminados em **-y**, **-le**, **-er**, **-ow**, **-some**.

3. Particularidades do aspecto gráfico

happy	happier	happiest
hot [hɔt] (quente)	hotter	hottest
late	later	latest

Nos adjectivos terminados em **-y** precedido de consoante, este passa a **-i**; nos adjectivos terminados numa só consoante precedida de uma só vogal, dobra-se a consoante; nos adjectivos terminados em **-e** mudo, este cai.

4. Os graus precedidos de «more» e «most»

a) interesting,	**more** interesting,	**most** interesting
b) careful,	**more** careful,	**most** careful

Fazem-se preceder de **more** e **most**:
a) os adjectivos de três ou mais sílabas,
b) os adjectivos dissilábicos acentuados na primeira sílaba, (excepto os referidos em 5B2c).

5. Graus irregulares

good [gud]	better ['betə]	best [best]	bom
bad [bæd]	worse [wə:s]	worst [wə:st]	mau
little ['litl]	less [les]	least [li:st]	pouco
little ['litl] small [smɔ:l]	smaller ['smɔ:lə]	smallest ['smɔ:list]	pequeno
much [mʌtʃ] many ['meni]	more [mɔ:]	most [məust]	muito, -a muitos, -as

6. Graus com dupla forma

> The **next** street to the left is the **nearest** to Jane's office.
> Please, give me the **latest** edition of the Financial Times.
> – Here is the **last** copy (['kɔpi] Exemplar).
> John went **farther** into the streets of the City.
> Jane answered **further** letters.

Alguns adjectivos têm duas formas de comparativo, com possível diferença de significado:

near [niə] perto, próximo	nearer ['niərə] mais perto	nearest ['niərist] o mais próximo (distância) next [nekst] o seguinte (sequência)
late [leit] tarde, atrasado	later ['leitə] mais tarde latter ['lætə] este último (de dois)	latest ['leitist] o mais tarde (tempo) last [la:st] o último (sequência)
far [fa:] longe, afastado	farther ['fa:ðə] mais longe further ['fə:ðə] mais longe, subsequente	farthest ['fa:ðist] o mais longe (distância) furthest [fə:ðist] o mais afastado (sentido conotativo)

7. Comparação

> Mr. Holdstock is **as** kind **as** he is polite.
> There are **not so** / **not as** many people now as there are during the rush-hours.
> Jane is la**ter than** yesterday.
> **The** longer [lɔŋgə] she works, **the** later she gets home.

O comparativo de igualdade forma-se com **as – as,** na forma negativa com **not so – as** ou **not as – as**.
O comparativo de superioridade ou de inferioridade é seguido de **than** (do que).
A dependência no comparativo é expressa por **the – the** (quanto mais – tanto mais).

Exercícios 5 C

1. Fixe os seguintes adjectivos e forme os respectivos graus de comparativo e superlativo:

big	[big]	grande
busy	['bizi]	ocupado, trabalhador
comfortable	['kʌmfətəbl]	confortável
delighted	[di'laitid]	encantado
early	['əːli]	cedo
easy	['iːzi]	fácil
elegant	['eligənt]	elegante
exciting	[ik'saitiŋ]	excitante
famous	['feiməs]	célebre
gay	[gei]	alegre
gentle	['dʒentl]	gentil; distinto
glorious	['glɔːriəs]	magnífico
honest	['ɔnist]	honesto
important	[im'pɔːtənt]	importante
large	[laːdʒ]	grande
long	[lɔŋ]	comprido
lovely	['lʌvli]	encantador
marvellous	['maːvələs]	maravilhoso
necessary	['nesisəri]	necessário

pretty	['priti]	bonito
rainy	['reini]	chuvoso
simple	['simpl]	simples
splendid	['splendid]	esplêndido
thin	[θin]	fino, delgado
tired	['taiəd]	fatigado
wonderful	['wʌndəful]	maravilhoso

2. Complete as seguintes frases com os graus adequados dos adjectivos:
   a) Jane is early, Father is ____, but Mother is the ____ of all.
   b) The Mansion House is interesting, the Bank of England is ____, but the Stock Exchange is ____.
   c) Toast is good, cornflakes are ____, but the ____ breakfast is bacon and eggs.

3. De cada uma das frases seguintes, forme duas, de acordo com o exemplo apresentado:
   Father's breakfast is bigger than Jane's.
   Jane's breakfast is not so (not as) big as Father's.
   a) Jane's work ____ Mr. Holdstock's work (easy)
   b) Helen's coat ____ Jane's coat (elegant)
   c) dining-room ____ John's room (beautiful)
   d) the streets of the City ____ the streets of Wood Green (crowded)
   e) the letter from France ____ the letter from Liverpool (important)
   f) the Bank of England ____ the Mansion House (famous)

4. Complete as seguintes frases de acordo com o exemplo apresentado:
   Mr. Holdstock is as careful as Jane.
   a) Jane ____ Mother (busy)
   b) John's work ____ Father's work (important)
   c) Mother ____ Jane (pretty)
   d) the Mansion House ____ the Bank of England (splendid)
   e) John ____ Jane (gay)

5. Complete as seguintes frases com o grau do adjectivo apropriado:
   a) near: I'm late. Which is the ____ way to the station? Jane takes the ____ letter.
   b) late: This is the ____ letter for today. Father gets the ____ copy of the Times. The ____ edition of the Guardian is very interesting.
   c) far: John's place of work is ____ than Jane's. There are no ____ letters.

At the Post Office

Texto **6 A**

The Manager at Jane's office, Mr. Morrow, sends for her. She knocks at his door and he calls: «Come in!»
«Good morning, Mr. Morrow», she says. «What do you want me to do?»
«I want you to go to the post office and buy some stamps. We need a hundred 28p stamps, a hundred and fifty $20\frac{1}{2}$p stamps and two hundred 16p stamps. Also the usual money orders – let's say a hundred. Then have these two letters registered. Take this cheque with you and have it changed for money at our bank».
«Anything else, Mr. Morrow?»
«Yes, before you leave, ask Mr. Holdstock to phone Mr. McDowell and tell him that I should like to see him. Say that I shall expect him on the fifth, that is the day after tomorrow, at 9.30.»

It is only a short walk to the post office. Jane goes in and walks to one of the positions at the counter. Usually there are a larger number of people waiting. But this morning Jane seems to be lucky. There is no one else waiting at this position. So she waits a few minutes, but no clerk comes to her. Much annoyed, she goes two positions farther down the counter and waits again angrily, in a long queue this time. When her turn finally comes she asks the clerk: «Why is no one serving at that position there?»
The clerk answers in a rather unfriendly manner: «Can't you see the notice? It says 'Position Closed'.»

Jane is greatly surprised. «I'm sorry», she says. «I must have completely overlooked it.»
Now she buys her stamps and the money orders, and has the letters registered. She is about to return to the office when she remembers: before she leaves the post office she must telephone a boyfriend. He may possibly want to go out with her tonight.
Jane goes into a call-box and takes off the receiver. She puts a 5p coin into the slot and dials the number, 297-0958. When she hears the pay-tone she quickly presses the coin, and the connection is through. After the call she walks back to her office.

Notas gramaticais **6 B**

1. O imperativo

> **Come** in!
> «**Take** this cheque with you», says Mr. Holdstock.
> Father asks John: «Please, **give** me the newspaper.»

O Imperativo tem a mesma forma para o singular e plural: *Come in!* = «entra!», «entre!», «entrem!». Tem a **forma do Infinito sem to**. Só se usa o ponto de exclamação quando se trata de facto de uma exclamação.

2. Adjectivo e advérbio

> Jane is **angry**. She speaks in an **angry** voice.*
> ([vɔis] voz)
> She speaks **angrily**.

Um adjectivo (*angry*) qualifica um substantivo (*Jane, voice*).
Um advérbio (*angrily*) refere-se a um verbo (*speaks*), um adjectivo ou um advérbio.

---
* Em inglês o adjectivo qualificativo é invariável em género e número e precede o substantivo que qualifica. (*N.T.*)

3. Os advérbios simples

> Jane **almost** forgot to telephone.
> Why is no one serving **there**?
> **Then** have this letter registered.

Existe uma série de advérbios simples de modo (*almost*), de lugar (*there*) e de tempo (*then*). Só alguns são susceptíveis de formar graus, como por exemplo *soon* ([suːn] em breve) (vd. 6B8).

4. Os advérbios derivados

> Jane quick**ly** presses the coin.
> He may possib**ly** want to go out with her.
> She waits ang**rily**.

Na sua maioria, os advérbios formam-se juntando o sufixo *-ly* a um adjectivo: *quick – quickly*.

Nos adjectivos terminados em *-le* após consoante, esta terminação passa a *-ly*: *possible – possibly*.

Nos adjectivos terminados em *-y* precedido de consoante, aquele passa a *-i*: *angry – angrily*.

Quando três *l* se encontram só dois se mantêm: *full* ([ful] cheio, pleno) + *ly – fully*.

Atenção às seguintes particularidades gráficas:

tru**e** ([truː] verdadeiro)	–	truly
whol**e** ([həu] total)	–	wholly
large (['lɑːdʒ])	–	largely

Em *true* e *whole* cai o *-e* mudo final; em *large* mantém-se.

5. Perífrase adverbial

> The clerk is **unfriendly**.
> He answers **in an unfriendly manner**.

Os adjectivos terminados em *-ly* formam o advérbio por meio de uma perífrase com **in a ... manner** ou **in a ... way**.

São entre outros:

	friendly ['frendli]	simpático
	lovely ['lʌvli]	encantador, amoroso
	brotherly ['brʌðəli]	fraternal
	manly ['mænli]	viril

6. Adjectivos e advérbios com a mesma forma

> A **daily** newspaper comes **daily**.

Algumas determinações temporais em *-ly* são usadas como adjectivo e como advérbio:

early ['əːli]	cedo	weekly ['wiːkli]	semanal
hourly ['auəli]	por hora	monthly ['mʌnθli]	mensal
daily ['deili]	diário	yearly ['jəːli]	anual

7. Advérbios com dupla forma

> He works **hard**.   Ele trabalha duramente.
> He **hardly** works. Ele pouco trabalha.

Alguns adjectivos são usados como advérbio sem qualquer alteração. Mas têm também uma forma adverbial com o sufixo *-ly*, que tem no entanto outro significado.

Adjectivo + Advérbio	Advérbio
hard duro, difícil	**hardly** mal, apenas
short curto	**shortly** recentemente
high alto	**highly** extremamente

8. Graus dos advérbios

> soon   – soon**er**   – soon**est**
> happily – **more** happily – **most** happily

Os advérbios simples – na medida em que podem ter graus (vd. 6B3) – formam-nos com *–er*, *-est*; os derivados formam-nos com *more*, *most*. Os graus irregulares dos adjectivos também servem de advérbio (vd. 5B5 GRAUS IRREGULARES).

9. O advérbio «muito»

> Mr. Morrow is **very** busy.
> Jane was **much/very** annoyed.
> We thank you **very much**.

Para adjectivos e advérbios usa-se **very**. Junto de verbos, a par de **much**, está a usar-se cada vez mais *very*; a ênfase expressa-se com **very much**.

Exercícios 6 C

1. Forme advérbios a partir dos seguintes adjectivos:
   wonderful, gay, pretty, comfortable, beautiful, good, yearly, busy, polite, large, whole, lovely, necessary, early, gentle, easy, glorious, simple.
2. Substitua as palavras portuguesas por inglesas:
   Many people (depressa) leave Bank Station. (Quase) all of them are clerks. Jane is late; she (irritadamente) hurries down Princess Street. When she is not (cedo) she is always (irritada). The streets of the City are (muito) crowded. Mr. Holdstock is very (simpático). He answers Jane (com simpatia). He speaks French (bem). His German (também) is (bom). (Hoje) Jane has to go to the (próximo) post office. It is (só) a short walk. The clerk is a very (antipático) man. He answers Jane (de modo antipático). She (quase) forgets to phone her boyfriend. It is (já) half past nine.

Let's Have Lunch

Texto 7 A

It is one o'clock. Jane finishes typing a letter and puts it in an envelope. Mr. Holdstock looks up from his work.
«Well», he says, «what about lunch?»
«All right», Jane answers, «let's go.»
They leave the building and go down the street to a nearby café. Jane usually has lunch there because the

food is inexpensive. They find an empty table in a corner and sit down. They study the menu. A waitress comes up. Jane orders some soup and a salad. Mr. Holdstock asks for some sandwiches and a piece of cheese.

During the meal Mr. Holdstock talks about his weekend plans.

He intends to go up the river Thames as far as Windsor and visit the castle.

«We are expecting a visitor», says Jane. «A young man from Germany is coming next Saturday to stay with us for some weeks while he takes an English course.»

Having finished their lunch they ask the waitress to make out their bills. Jane takes her money out of her bag. There are some pound notes and some coins: a fifty-pence piece, several ten-pence pieces and some five-pence pieces. These are all nickel coins. Jane has some copper coins too: two-pence pieces, pennies and a halfpenny.

«I expect», Jane says, «our German visitor will find English money quite easy to understand, now we have the decimal system, with a hundred new pence in the pound.»
«Yes», Mr. Holdstock replies. «Our old money system was rather difficult for most foreigners. There were twenty shillings in a pound, twelve old pence in a shilling and four farthings in a penny.»
«Yes», Jane adds, «and there was also the halfcrown, which was two shillings and six old pence.»
They get their bills, and put a little money beside their plates as a tip for the waitress. Then they pay at the desk and leave the café.

Notas gramaticais 7 B

1. Os numerais cardinais

> There are **a hundred** pence in a pound.

A hundred é um numeral cardinal.
Os numerais cardinais mais importantes são:

0	*como valor numérico*	naught	[nɔːt]
	em números telefónicos	o	[əu]
	como ponto de uma escala	zero	[ˈziɔrəu]
	como sinal gráfico	cipher	[ˈsaifə]

1	one	[wʌn]	13	thirteen	[ˈθəːˈtiːn]
2	two	[tuː]	14	fourteen	[ˈfɔːˈtiːn]
3	three	[θriː]	15	fifteen	[ˈfifˈtiːn]
4	four	[fɔː]	16	sixteen	[ˈsiksˈtiːn]
5	five	[faiv]	17	seventeen	[ˈsevnˈtiːn]
6	six	[siks]	18	eighteen	[ˈeiˈtiːn]
7	seven	[ˈsevn]	19	nineteen	[ˈnainˈtiːn]
8	eight	[eit]	20	twenty	[ˈtwenti]
9	nine	[nain]	21	twenty-one	[ˈtwentiˈwʌn]
10	ten	[ten]	22	twenty-two	[ˈtwentiˈtuː]
11	eleven	[iˈlevn]	23	twenty-three	[ˈtwentiˈθriː]
12	twelve	[twelv]	24	twenty-four	[ˈtwentiˈfɔː]

30 thirty	['θəːti]	70 seventy	['sevnti]
40 forty	['fɔːti]	80 eighty	['eiti]
50 fifty	['fifti]	90 ninety	['nainti]
60 sixty	['siksti]	99 ninety-nine	['nainti'nain]

100	a hundred	[ə 'hʌndrəd]
	one hundred	['wʌn 'hʌndrəd]
101	one hundred and one	
158	one hundred and fifty-eight	
200	two hundred	
1,000	a thousand	[ə 'θauzənd]
	one thousand	['wʌn 'θauzənd]
1,583	one thousand five hundred and eighty-three	
2,000	two thousand	
100,000	one hundred thousand	
1,000,000	a million	[ə 'miljən]
	one million	['wʌn 'miljən]
1,000,000,000	*Brit. Engl.* a/one thousand million(s)	
	Amer. Engl. a/one billion	['biljən]

2. Particularidades dos numerais cardinais

a) fifteen ['fif'tiːn] – fifteen pence ['fiftiːn 'pens]

Nos números **thirteen** a **nineteen** ambas as sílabas são acentuadas. Mas se a um destes numerais se seguir um substantivo acentuado na primeira sílaba, só é acentuada a primeira sílaba.

b) one thousand four hundred **and** forty-five

As dezenas ligam-se às unidades por **hífen**. O conjunto é ligado por **and** ao número que o antecede.

c) **a** hundred – **one** hundred and four

Hundred, **thousand**, **million** e **billion** são geralmente precedidos de **a**. Mas se se lhe seguir outro número são precedidos por **one**.

d) | three million**s** – two million three hundred thousand |

O numeral **million** tem plural quando substantivo, mas é invariável quando seguido de outros numerais.

e) | millions **of** people – thousands **of** pounds – hundreds **of** letters |

Millions, thousands e **hundreds** ligam-se a substantivos com a preposição **of** para designar quantidades indeterminadas.

f) | 1984 = nineteen (hundred and) eighty-four |

O número do ano lê-se indicando o grupo do milhar e centenas e depois o das dezenas e unidades.

3. «Pennies» e «pence»

> Jane has some **pennies** in her bag.
> There are a hundred **pence** in a pound.

A palavra **penny** tem duas formas de plural: **pennies** são um conjunto de moedas de um **penny** cada; **pence** é uma indicação global de valor ou preço.

4. Indicações de valor

Na lista que se segue estão as indicações mais importantes de valor e de preço:

Linguagem comum

a halfpenny [hɑːfˈpeni (ˈheipni)] = ½p (a ha'penny)
a penny = 1p (one 'p')
twopence [ˈtʌpəns] = 2p (two 'p')
fivepence [ˈfaivpəns] = 5p (five 'p')
  (para a moeda usa-se em linguagem popular *a bob* [bɔb])
tenpence [ˈtenpəns] = 10p (ten 'p') (two bob)
fifty pence [ˈfifti ˈpens] = 50p (fifty 'p') (ten bob)
one pound and seventy-five = £1.75 (one seventy-five)
  (pence [ˈwʌn ˈpaund ənd   O sinal de libra £ precede
  ˈsevnti ˈfaiv ˈpens]   sempre o número.

5. As horas

> ten (minutes) **past** three (o'clock) – ten (minutes) **to** one (o'clock) – **half** past nine.

Até aos 30 minutos usa-se a palavra **past** (depois) seguida da hora; depois dos 30 minutos usa-se **to** (para) também seguido da hora. Os quartos de hora exprimem-se com *a quarter to/past*.

> at four a.m. = às quatro da manhã
> at four p.m. = às quatro da tarde

Na linguagem comum usam-se apenas os números até doze, seguidos, se necessário, por **in the morning/a.m.** (do latim *ante meridiem* = antes do meio-dia) ou **in the afternoon/p.m.** (do latim *post meridiem* = depois do meio-dia).

> The train arrives at ten fourty-five.
> It is now 18.00 (eighteen hours).

Em horários de viagem e na indicação oficial das horas usam-se os números até vinte e quatro.

6. Particularidades na formação do plural

> a potat**o** ([pə'teitəu] = batata)   – some potat**oes**
> a radi**o** (['reidiəu]   = rádio)   – some radi**os**

Um conjunto de substantivos terminados em **-o** formam o plural acrescentando **-es**. O conjunto **-oes** pronuncia-se [-əuz]. Os substantivos terminados em *-o*, mas de origem estrangeira, seguem a regra geral, por ex. *zoos*.

Exercícios 7 C

1. Escreva por extenso os numerais de 1 a 23, de 48 a 50, as dezenas, 100, 1000, 1525 e leia-os.

2. Leia as seguintes horas (em linguagem comum e oficial): 13.05, 8.30, 21.35, 2.05, 11.50, 12.45, 10.30, 21.04, 7.55, 9.30, 6.15, 18.45, 19.30, 3.55, 9.25, 17.40.
3. Leia: 1p, 5p, $^1/_2$p, 50p, £1.65, £3.90, 10p, £437.75.

Writing a Letter

Texto **8 A**

The prospect of meeting a young man from Germany for the first time pleases Jane, and she wants to be helpful to him. So she decides to write to the London Tourist Board for him. She writes from her home address and this is her letter:

                         64, Eastern Avenue,
                                  Wood Green,
                                    London N. 22
                                    20th May, 19..

The London Tourist Board,
4, Grosvenor Gardens SW1W ODU

Dear Sirs,
Could you please send me any information you have about things to see and do in London which are of interest to young people from abroad? I believe you issue leaflets on this subject in various languages and I should like to have copies for a visitor from Germany who is coming to stay with us.
With thanks in advance for your attention to the matter, I am

                                    Yours faithfully,
                                    Jane Brown

Jane's letter is a formal letter addressed to the staff of an office. So it begins «Dear Sirs» and ends «Yours faithfully». Notice the comma after these two phrases. In a letter to an acquaintance Jane begins «Dear Mr. McDowell» and ends with «Yours sincerely», in a letter to a friend she begins «Dear Helen» and ends with «Yours». And on the envelope she puts «Miss Helen Gray» and «Mr. A. McDowell», or «A. McDowell Esq.» (Esquire).

The London Tourist Board supplies information on the London area. There is an English Tourist Board for information on other parts of England, as well as separate tourist boards for Scotland, Wales, Ireland and the Isle of Man. Travel advice for the whole of Britain is given by the British Tourist Authority at 64, St James's St, London SW1A 1NF.

Notas gramaticais **8 B**

1. Os numerais ordinais

> Jane is meeting him for the **first** time.
> This is the **eighth** lesson. (to meet [miːt] encontrar, ir ter com)

Além dos três primeiros numerais ordinais, todos os outros se formam a partir do cardinal, acrescentando **-th**. Em numerais compostos só o último algarismo toma esta terminação.

1st	**first** [fəːst]	11th	eleventh
2nd	**second** ['sekənd]	12th	twelfth
3rd	**third** [θəːd]	13th	thirteenth
4th	fourth [fɔːθ]	14th	fourteenth
5th	fifth [fifθ]	15th	fifteenth
6th	sixth [siksθ]	16th	sixteenth
7th	seventh ['sevnθ]	17th	seventeenth
8th	**eighth** [eitθ]	18th	eighteenth
9th	ninth [nainθ]	19th	nineteenth
10th	tenth	20th	twent**ie**th ['twentiiθ]

21st	twenty-**first**	70th	seventieth ['sevntiiθ]
22**nd**	twenty-**second**	80th	eightieth ['eitiiθ]
23**rd**	twenty-**third**	90th	ninetieth ['naintiiθ]
24th	twenty-fourth	100th	the (one) hundredth ['hʌndrədθ]
30th	thirtieth ['θəːtiiθ]	101st	the hundred and first
40th	fortieth ['fɔːtiiθ]	135th	the hundred and thirty-fifth
50th	fiftieth ['fiftiiθ]		
60th	sixtieth ['sikstiiθ]	1000th	the thousandth

2. A data

a)
> 18th May(,) 1984
> lê-se: **the** eighteenth **of** May nineteen (hundred and) eighty-four

b)
> May 18(th), 1984
> lê-se: May **the** eighteenth...

Antes do número do ano coloca-se uma vírgula que, no entanto, muitas vezes não se usa na forma *a)*. Na data, os ordinais aparecem muitas vezes sem terminação (*-st, -nd, -rd, -th*).

3. Números fraccionários

> $1/2$ = a half [hɑːf]　　　　$2/3$ = two third**s**
> $1/4$ = a quarter ['kwɔːtə]　$3/4$ = three quarter**s**
> $1/5$ = a fifth　　　　　　　$4/5$ = four fitths [fifθs]

Nos **números fraccionários** o numerador tem a forma do cardinal e o denominador a do ordinal. Se o numerador for maior do que 1, o denominador toma a forma do plural.

> 4·378 lê-se: four point [pɔint] (ou: decimal
> ['desiməl]) – three – seven – eight
> 0·215 lê-se: point – two – one – five

Nos **números decimais** a unidade é assinalada com um ponto (e não uma vírgula). Esse ponto é por vezes colocado em posição elevada.

4. Números frequentativos

> once [wʌns] = uma vez   four **times** = quatro vezes
> twice [twais] = duas vezes   five **times** = cinco vezes
> three **times** = três vezes   etc.

5. Os dias da semana, os meses, as estações do ano

The days of the week

Sunday	['sʌndi]	domingo	**Thursday**	['θəːzdi]	quinta-feira
Monday	['mʌndi]	segunda-feira	**Friday**	['fraidi]	sexta-feira
Tuesday	['tjuːzdi]	terça-feira	**Saturday**	['sætədi]	sábado
Wednesday	['wenzdi]	quarta-feira			

The months [mʌnθs]

January	[dzænjuəri]		**July**	[dzu(ː)'lai]
February	['februəri]		**August**	['ɔːgəst]
March	[maːtʃ]		**September**	[sep'tembə]
April	['eipril]		**October**	[ɔk'təubə]
May	[mei]		**November**	[nəu'vembə]
June	[dʒuːn]		**December**	[di'sembə]

Os nomes dos dias da semana e dos meses escrevem-se sempre com maiúscula.

The seasons ['siːznz]

spring	[spriŋŋ]	Primavera	**autumn**	['ɔːtəm]	Outono
summer	['sʌmə]	Verão	**winter**	['wintə]	Inverno

6. Particularidades na formação do plural

leaf	[liːf]	–	lea**ves**	[liːvz]	folha
thief	[θiːf]	–	thie**ves**	[θiːvz]	ladrão
calf	[kɑːf]	–	cal**ves**	[kɑːvz]	vitela
half	[hɑːf]	–	hal**ves**	[hɑːvz]	metade
shelf	[ʃelf]	–	shel**ves**	[ʃelvz]	prateleira
self	[self]	–	sel**ves**	[selvz]	próprio
wolf	[wulf]	–	wol**ves**	[wulvz]	lobo
life	[laif]	–	li**ves**	[laivz]	vida
knife	[naif]	–	kni**ves**	[naivz]	faca
wife	[waif]	–	wi**ves**	[waivz]	esposa

Uma série de palavras terminadas em **-f, -fe** forma o plural em **-ves** [-vz]. (Atenção à pronúncia.)

Exercícios 8 C

1. Escreva por extenso e leia os seguintes numerais ordinais, fraccionários e decimais: o 1.º, 2.º, 3.º, 5.º, 8.º, 12.º, 14.º, 20.º, 40.º, 101.º; $^1/_2$, $^1/_4$, $^3/_5$, $^2/_3$, $^3/_4$, $^1/_{10}$, $^1/_{12}$, $^1/_{100}$, $^1/_{1000}$, $^1/_{1000000}$; 3.4, 1.5, 2.603, 0.2, 0.02.

2. Complete as seguintes frases:
   Spring begins on... (21 de Março)
   Summer begins on... (21 de Junho)
   Autumn begins on... (23 de Setembro)
   Winter begins on... (22 de Dezembro)
   The day after Tuesday is...
   The day before Sunday is...
   Today is... (por ex., quarta-feira, 6 de Novembro de 19...)
   Yesterday was...
   I was born on... (was born [wəz 'bɔːn] = nasci)
   My mother was born on...
   My father was born on...

3. Construa frases com o plural das seguintes palavras: house, room, garage, secretary, journey, work, basin, toothbrush, manager, egg, carriage, office, potato, radio, wife, half, leaf.

The Browns' Home

Texto **9 A**

When John Brown arrived home in his car after a hard day's work at the garage it was already half past six. He parked the car in the road outside the house, opened the gate and walked through the garden to the front door.

John opened the door with his key and called to his mother:

«Hullo, Mother. Is dinner ready? I'm hungry.»

«Hullo, John», she answered, «It's nearly ready. I'll call you.»

John went upstairs to his room.

The house had two storeys, the ground floor and the upstairs floor. On the ground floor were the lounge, the dining-room and the kitchen. Upstairs there were four bedrooms and a bathroom.

John opened the window and looked into the garden. There was a lawn, surrounded by bushes. In one corner there was his sister Jane, sitting on a garden seat. John picked up a book and started to read. Then he suddenly heard his mother's voice.
«Dinner is ready now, John», she called.
John shut the window, left his room and went downstairs again to the dining-room. On the way he passed the lounge with its armchairs, settee and fireplace. Above the fireplace there were some family photographs, a clock and vases with flowers.
The Browns liked the house very much. They had lived in a flat in town for some years so they were glad to live in a suburb now and to have a garden round the house. The new house was more expensive than their old flat but they expected to remain in it for a long time.
Then John opened the door of the dining-room and went in to join his family for dinner.

Notas gramaticais **9 B**

1. O pretérito (past tense) dos verbos fracos

> John open**ed** the gate

O **pretérito** (Past Tense [ˈpɑːst tens]) de *to open* é *opened*. É uma forma única para todas as pessoas, tanto no singular como no plural. Os verbos que formam o pretérito com a terminação **-ed** chamam-se fracos.

2. O particípio passado (past participle) dos verbos fracos

> They had liv**ed** in town for some years

Os verbos cujo pretérito termina em **-ed** têm esta mesma terminação no **particípio passado** (*Past Participle* ['pɑːst 'pɑːtisipl]).
O INFINITO (to live), o PRETÉRITO (lived) e o PARTICÍPIO PASSADO (lived) são as FORMAS PRINCIPAIS do verbo, das quais derivam todas as outras.

3. Pronúncia de -ed

> John arrived [d]
> John walked [t]
> John expected [id]

A terminação *-ed* pronuncia-se do seguinte modo:
  depois de sons sonoros [d],
  depois de sons surdos [t],
  depois de «d» e «t» [id]

4. Particularidades gráficas

> to cry [krai] (= chorar)   – cried
> to step [step] (= andar, pisar) – stepped
> to like   – liked

Ao acrescentar *-ed* o *-y* precedido de consoante passa a *-i-*; uma consoante final precedida de uma só vogal acentuada é dobrada; um *-e* mudo final desaparece. (vd. Particularidades do aspecto gráfico 5B3.)

5. Verbos fracos irregulares

> to say   [sei]   said   [sed]   said   [sed]
> to hear [hiə]   heard [həːd] heard [həːd]
> to leave [liːv] left   [left] left   [left]
> to shut [ʃʌt]   shut   [ʃʌt]   shut   [ʃʌt]

Em alguns verbos fracos, a terminação *-ed* tomou a forma de **-d** ou **-t**. Por vezes também se modificou a vogal do radical.

6. O pretérito (past tense) de «to be»

> It **was** half past six.
> Upstairs there **were** four bedrooms.

As formas do pretérito de *to be* são **was** [wɔz, wəz] e **were** [wə(ː)]:

I	was	eu	era, estava fui, estive	we		nós	éramos, estávamos fomos, estivemos
you	**were**	tu você	eras, estavas foste, estiveste era, estava foi, esteve	you	were	vós vocês	éreis, estáveis fostes, estivestes eram, estavam foram, estiveram
he **she** **it**	**was**	ele ela	era, estava foi, esteve	they		eles elas	eram, estavam foram, estiveram

7. O pretérito (past tense) de «to have»

> The house **had** two storeys.

A forma do pretérito de *to have* é **had** [hæd, həd]; é igual para todas as pessoas, tanto no singular como no plural: *I had* eu tinha, eu tive; *you had* tu tinhas, tu tiveste, você tinha, você teve, etc.

8. Particularidades da formação do plural

> child [tʃaild]   – child**ren** [ˈtʃildrən] criança
> ox   [ɔks]   – ox**en** [ˈɔksən] boi

Exercícios 9 C

Ponha as seguintes frases no Past Tense. Dê atenção às particularidades gráficas! Leia o que escreveu! (Todos os verbos que não foram apresentados nos números 5 a 7 das notas gramaticais, são fracos regulares.)

1. Jane Brown is a secretary. She works with Johnson and Howard. Their office is near the Bank of England. John and Jane Brown live

at Wood Green. The house belongs to their parents. John has a room of his own. It is on the upstairs floor. Jane needs half an hour to get to her office.
2. John Brown is at breakfast. In front of him there is a cup and a saucer. John asks his mother for another cup of tea. She pours tea in his cup. John has some cornflakes and toast. It is a very quick breakfast. Father has some bacon and eggs. He helps himself to a cup of tea.
3. Jane arrives at Bank Station. Many people leave the station with her. As she is later than yesterday she hurries down the street. The streets of the City are crowded. In the evening they are almost deserted. Jane passes the Mansion House. She enters the office of Johnson and Howard.

An Evening at Home

Texto **10 A**

One of the best-known English sayings is «An Englishman's home is his castle». The English are very fond of their homes, and this includes the Browns. Let's see what the family did yesterday. When John came downstairs from his room he went into the dining-room and sat down at the table.
«Hello, everyone», he said.
Mother gave the family their meal and they began to eat. The evening meal, generally taken after seven o'clock and called «dinner», is the principal meal in most English families on weekdays. The lighter midday meal is called «lunch». On Sundays the main meal is taken at midday and may be called either «lunch» or «dinner». There is also the name «supper» for a late evening meal, lighter than dinner.
Family tastes in eating vary greatly, but a full meal may start with soup, followed by a main course of fish or

meat, and end with a sweet (often called «pudding»), cheese or fruit.

Having finished diner, Father and Mother went into the lounge to watch TV (television) while Jane sat at the table and wrote a letter to a friend in Edinburgh. The Browns had a new colour television set on wich they could receive six different channels. They found details of the programmes in their newspapers, and in the weeklies published by the BBC and ITV.

John chose to go upstairs to his room again. He wanted to listen to pop music on his stereo recordplayer, which he could regulate to any pitch. He also had his own transistor radio and a tape-recorder, and could record his favourite music «off the air». It was past midnight when John went to bed.

Notas gramaticais **10 B**

1. O pretérito (past tense) dos verbos fortes

> They **began** to eat.

O pretérito do *to begin* é *began*. Os verbos como *to begin* que formam o pretérito (e o particípio passado) **modificando a vogal do radical** chamam-se verbos fortes.

2. O particípio passado (past participle) dos verbos fortes

> The meal **taken** about seven o'clock is the principal meal

(à letra: A refeição tomada cerca das sete horas é a principal.)
O particípio passado de *to take* é *taken*.

Não há regra nenhuma para as formas principais dos verbos fortes (por ex.: *to take*, *took*, *taken*). Por isso recomenda-se que eles sejam estudados como se se tratasse de vocabulário.

3. O pretérito (past tense) dos verbos auxiliares

> John could **record** his favourite music.

Nesta frase *could* é o pretérito de *can*. *Can* é um dos **verbos defectivos**, que não têm Infinito, nem Imperativo, nem Particípio Passado; têm apenas uma forma para o Presente e uma para o Pretérito. Esses verbos são:

can	[kæn, kən]	**could**	[kud, kəd]	poder, saber (+ Infinito)
will	[will]	**would**	[wud, wəd]	querer
shall	[ʃæl, ʃəl]	**should**	[ʃud, ʃəd]	dever
may	[mei]	**might**	[mait]	poder, ter licença de, ser possível
must	[mʌst, məst]	**must**	[mʌst, məst]	ter de, ter que

Os **verbos auxiliares normais** *to be* (ser ou estar) e *to have* (ter) têm as formas principais:

to be [bi(ː)]	**was/were** [wɔz, wəz/wə(ː)]	**been** [bi(ː)n]
to have [hæv, həv]	**had** [hæd, həd]	**had**

4. O substituto «one»

a) Here are some records. Which **one** would (=gostarias) you like to hear? – A new **one**, please.
The Browns' house has three large rooms and several smaller **ones**.

Em geral, um substantivo cuja repetição se pretende evitar é substituído pela palavra **one**. Se o substantivo estiver no plural usa-se a forma de plural **ones**.

b)
> This is my friend's car, that is my **own**.
> There is cold **water** as well as warm.
> John's friend has two sisters, John only **one**.
> Can I have a copy of The Times? – Here's the **latest**.

Em geral, não se usa esta palavra:
  depois de *own*,
  para nomes designativos de matéria,
  depois de numerais usados como adjectivos,
  depois de superlativos.

6. Preposições

O estudo das preposições inglesas faz-se com melhor resultado se as aprendermos em expressões, ligadas a vocábulos. Nesta e nas lições seguintes vamos apresentar preposições usadas em acepções diversas, com exemplos elucidativos. Muitas vezes as preposições são usadas como advérbios nas expressões apresentadas.

As preposições podem referir lugar (l.), tempo (t.) ou conotação (c.):

> **about** l.: John walked **about** the garden. (pelo)
>   t.: Jane is **about** twenty-six. (cerca de, mais ou menos)
>   c.: Mr. Brown tells us **about** London. (sobre [um tema])

Em geral, as preposições precedem um substantivo ou um pronome pessoal complemento.

I have no money about me	não tenho dinheiro comigo
about this time	mais ou menos a esta hora
he looks about him	ele olha à sua volta
what is it about?	de que se trata?
I'll see about it	eu vou tratar disso

Exercícios　　**10 C**

Construa frases com os verbos fortes do texto no presente e passe-as depois para o pretérito.

At the Airport

Texto **11 A**

«Where is the letter from Karl, Mother, the letter that came yesterday? I can't remember when his plane arrives.»

«As far as I remember, Karl said the arrival time was about 4 o'clock. But I'm not sure whether that was the time at the airport or at the air terminal in London. Anyhow, there's his letter on the table, John.»

«Thanks. Ah yes, 4 o'clock is the time he is due at London Airport. He won't reach the air terminal til nearly an hour later. I think I'll go and meet him at the airport in the car. He has never been in London before and he may get lost if I don't pick him up.»

While John is driving to the airport he thinks of a visit he made to Germany last year. It was a wonderful experience for him and he learnt a lot.

At Heathrow John parks his car and makes his way into the airport building. Inside he finds the TV screens giving the arrival times of the planes. It is another ten minutes until Karl's flight is due. John has come early.

To pass the time John goes to the snack-bar for a cup of tea. He is thirsty. Suddenly he hears the number of Karl's plane on the loudspeaker. It has just arrived. So John hurries back to the exit gate. He soon sees Karl coming through the gate, carrying his bags. He recognises him from a photograph in Karl's letter.

«You must be Karl Schmidt. I'm John Brown. Welcome to England.»

«Hello, John. Thank you.»

«I hope you had a good flight.»

«Yes, thank you. It was very quick.»

«Let me take one of your bags. My car is outside.»

The two young men walk to the car. «By the way», John says as they go, «if you want some money changed there are branches of the main banks in the entrance hall. I think the rates of exchange are nearly the same everywhere.»

«No thanks. I had some money changed in Germany before I left.»

«All right then, let's go.» And so they drive off.

Notas gramaticais

1. Formação e emprego dos tempos

O presente (*Present Tense* ['preznt tens]) e o pretérito (*Past Tense*) são os chamados **tempos simples**. Formam-se a partir do infinito: *I begin – I began.*
Para a formação dos **tempos compostos** usam-se – como em português – verbos auxiliares. Para a formação do pretérito perfeito composto (*Present Perfect* ['preznt 'pəːfikt]) e do pretérito mais que perfeito (*Past Perfect* ['pɑːst 'pəːfikt]) usa-se sempre o verbo *to have*: *I have begun – I had begun.*

Tempos simples		*Tempos compostos*	
Present Tense Presente	**Past Tense** Pretérito	**Present Perfect** Pretérito composto	**Past perfect** Pretérito mais que perfeito
I begin eu começo	**I began** eu começava eu comecei	**I have begun** eu comecei eu tenho começado	**I had begun** eu começara eu tinha começado
I am eu sou eu estou	**I was** eu era eu fui eu estava eu estive	**I have been** eu tenho sido eu fui eu tenho estado eu estive	**I had been** eu tinha sido eu fora eu tinha estado eu estivera
I have eu tenho	**I had** eu tinha eu tive	**I have had** eu tenho tido eu tive	**I had had** eu tinha tido eu tivera

Portanto, o Present Perfect e o Past Perfect formam-se com um tempo do verbo **to have** + Past Participle (particípio passado) (Para o futuro vd. 12B1-5.).

2. Emprego do present tense

a) Seven plus [plʌs] seven **is** fourteen.
b) The bathroom **lies** on the other side of the landing.
c) They **have** breakfast at eight o'clock.
d) John **is** thirsty.

O Present Tense exprime afirmações intemporais (a), estados de duração ilimitada (b) e acções usuais (c). Também se pode expressar um estado no presente (d) (vd. a forma progressiva, 13B2).

3. Emprego do Past Tense

> Karl's letter **came** yesterday.
> Last year John **made** a visit to Germany.
> His visit to Germany **was** a wonderful experience.
> When he was there he **learnt** a lot.

O Past Tense exprime uma acção passada que não tem relação com o presente. As expressões adverbiais como *yesterday* (ontem), *last year* (o ano passado), *last week* (a semana passada), *last month* (o mês passado), *a week ago* (há uma semana), etc., exigem o emprego do Past Tense.

«Three years ago I **was** in London for six weeks.»

4. Emprego do Present Perfect

> John **has come** early.
> The plane **has** just **arrived**.
> Karl **has** never **been** in London.

O Present Perfect exprime uma acção que, tendo começado no passado, continua ou faz-se sentir no presente. Por isso, o Present Perfect liga-se a expressões adverbiais como *already* (já), *yet* (ainda), *just* (precisamente, agora mesmo), *this week*, *this month*, *this year*, *today*. Estas últimas expressões referem-se a um espaço de tempo que ainda não terminou.

«How long have you been in London?» (Há quanto tempo estás em Londres?) «I have been in London for six weeks now.» (Estou em Londres há seis semanas.)

5. Present Perfect e Past Tense

a) | I **have** never **seen** him. |

Tempo ilimitado e que continua; não o conheço.

b) | When I **was** in England last year, I never **saw** him. |

Durante a minha estadia, que já acabou, não o vi.
Em ligação com *ever* ['evə] alguma vez, *never* ['nevə] nunca, *sometimes* ['sʌmtaimz] às vezes, *often* ['ɔːfn] muitas vezes, *always* ['ɔːlweiz] sempre, *seldom* ['seldəm] poucas vezes, *rarely* [rɛəli] raramente, *frequently* ['friːkwəntli] frequentemente, emprega-se muitas vezes o Present Perfect, desde que a acção se venha prolongando até ao presente (a). Mas se houver na frase indicação de que não há relação com o presente, emprega-se o Past Tense (b).

desde as nove horas	(momento):	**since** nine o'clock
há três anos	(duração):	**for** three years
há dois dias	(duração):	**for** (**these**) two days

6. Emprego do Past Perfect

| I **had** just **come** to the station, when the train **arrived**. |

O Past Perfect exprime acções passadas antes de um determinado ponto do passado. Muitas vezes este tempo aparece em ligação com o Past Tense.

7. Lugar das expressões adverbiais na frase

(Para os advérbios vd. 6B2-9.)

a) | **This morning** Jane goes **to the manager**.
(Quando?)   (Onde)
Jane goes **to the manager this morning**.
      (Onde?)   (Quando?) |

Os **advérbios definidos** (de lugar e de tempo determinado) colocam-se no princípio ou no fim da frase. Se os dois se juntarem, o de lugar precede o de tempo.

a)
> Jane **quickly** goes to her office.
> (Jane goes to her office **quickly**.)
> (**Quickly** Jane goes to her office.)
> Karl has **just** arrived.

Os **advérbios indefinidos** (de modo e de tempo indeterminado) colocam-se entre o sujeito e o predicado com tempos simples; com tempos compostos colocam-se depois do auxiliar. (Só se colocam no princípio ou no fim da frase para lhes dar ênfase.)

Os advérbios de tempo indeterminado são, entre outros: *soon, then, often, never*, etc.

Um advérbio não pode separar o verbo do complemento directo. (vd. 27B3.)

8. Preposições

> Jane's office is **in** the City.
> She gets there **in** half an hour.
> Sometimes she is **in** a hurry.

× in

in l.: em, sobre, junto de
t.: em, a, perto de
c.: em, sobre, junto de, com

in a hurry ['hʌri]	com pressa
in the sky [skai]	no céu
in the street	na rua
in Fleet Street [fliːt]	na Fleet Street
in the field [fiːld]	no campo (pedaço de terreno)
in the country ['kʌntri]	no campo (por oposição à cidade)
in May	em Maio
in the evening	à tardinha, à noite
in the beginning [bi'giniŋ]	no princípio
in order ['ɔːdə]	por ordem, de modo a

in German	em alemão
in a word [wəːd]	numa palavra
in this way	deste modo

> Jane **goes** into the room.
> Yesterday she had to work far **into** the evening.
> Mr. Holdstock translates a letter **into** Spanish.
> [træns'leits] traduz

into

into l.: ⎫
      t.: ⎬ em, para dentro de
      c.: ⎭

to get into trouble ['trʌbl]	meter-se em dificuldades
to make ice [ais] into water	transformar gelo em água

> At Bank Station many people **get out** of the train.
> This typrwriter is **out of** date. ['aut əv 'deit] antiquada
> This book is **out of** print. ['aut əv 'print] esgotada

 out of

out of l.: fora de
       c.: a, em, de, sem

out of doors	ar livre
out of sight [sait]	fora do alcance da vista
out of reach [riːtʃ]	fora do alcance
made out of paper	feito de papel

9. Verbos fortes e fracos irregulares

Estude ou recapitule as formas principais dos seguintes verbos e construa frases nos diferentes tempos:

to meet	[iː]	**met**	[e]	**met**	[e]	encontrar
to drive	[ai]	**drove**	[əu]	**driven**	[i]	andar (num meio de transporte), conduzir
to get	[e]	**got**	[ɔ]	**got**	[ɔ]	obter, conseguir
to wake	[ei]	**woke**	[əu]	**woke(n)**	[əu]	despertar
to break	[ei]	**broke**	[əu]	**broken**	[əu]	partir, quebrar

Exercícios **11 C**

1. Forme o Past Tense, o Present Perfect e o Past Perfect de: he calls, we meet, you come, she sits, I write, you say, we hear, he arrives, we walk, they take.
2. Escolha 10 verbos e construa com cada um uma frase no Past Tense e outra no Present Perfect.
   Exemplo: to come
   > Karl **came** yesterday.
   > He **has** not **come** for a week.
3. Verifique nas frases seguintes se o verbo entre parêntesis deve ser usado no Past Tense ou no Present Perfect:
   Last year John __ in Germany. (to be)
   Karl __ in London since last Monday. (to be)
   I __ through the streets of London the whole week. (to walk)
   At the beginning of this week, I __ to Wood Green. (to go)
   I __ some English books yesterday. (to buy)
   I __ some books; here they are. (to buy)
   Last Monday Karl __ at London Airport. (to arrive)
   When I __ in London we __ to Windsor Castle. (to be, to go)
4. Construa frases nas quais apareçam os seguintes advérbios: already, yesterday, this week, a month ago, just.

A Walk in London

Texto **12 A**

«What are you going to do today, Karl?» Mr. Brown asks him on his first morning in England.

«I don't know. Can you suggest anything?»

«Would you like to go for a walk with me in Central London?»

«Yes, please.»

«Then we can take the underground and go to Piccadilly Circus. From there we shall be able to reach any part of the centre easily.»

They reach the station and catch a train.

At Piccadilly Circus they get out and walk over to the fountain. Here Karl admires the famous Eros statue on top of it.

There is nothing magnificent about the Circus, which has been called the «hub» of London, but it is fascinating in spite of its comparatively small size. Streams of people and traffic pour in and out of it from the six streets leading to the Circus – a dynamic and colourful picture.

Now Mr. Brown begins to explain. First he names some of the streets that lead to the Circus. «There is Regent Street, one of London's most fashionable shopping streets. There you will find many shops specialising in fine shoes and clothing. Another street leading off Piccadilly Circus is Shaftesbury Avenue, which goes in the direction of Soho.»

«What about that part, Mr. Brown?»

«It's the entertainment centre of London. You'll find all kinds of entertainment there: theatres, cinemas, nightclubs with cabarets, and restaurants and snackbars to suit every occasion and taste. It's London's most international quarter.»

«I suppose it's not so exciting in the daytime?»

«Well, it does have a charm of its own even in the daytime when there is a busy market in some of its back streets. But you're right. It doesn't really wake up until nightfall. You must go there one evening.»

While they talk, Mr. Brown and Karl walk down Haymarket to Trafalgar Square, and sit down on one of the benches around the fountains, watching the scores of pigeons. In the middle of the Square Nelson's Column rises high up into the air.

«Isn't that big building behind us the National Gallery?»

«Yes, it is. There you'll find works of art from almost every century and school of painting.»

«Are there also modern paintings and sculptures?»

«Yes, there are some. But we also have the Tate Gallery, which is reserved for modern art. You might like to visit that with Jane next week. She's very interested in art.»

«I know. She told me yesterday she would take me to some art galleries. And how about Whitehall, Mr. Brown, and the Houses of Parliament? Are we going to see that part today?»

«I hope so, unless it rains. But if we don't see it all today you will have other opportunities later, I promise you.»

«Thank you. I don't think I shall ever be at a loss for something to do in London, Mr. Brown.»

«No Karl. As our famous writer, Dr. Johnson, said: «When a man is tired of London he is tired of life.»

Notas gramaticais **12 B**

1. O Futuro (Future)

> We **shall be** able to reach the centre
> You **will have** other opportunities later.
> I hope you **will come** tomorrow.

Com poucas excepções, as acções futuras são expressas pelo verbo no futuro (*Future* [ˈfjuːtʃə]). Os verbos que exprimem uma esperança ou uma expectativa e por isso têm incidência no futuro (por ex. *to hope*, *to expect*, *to suppose*), também exigem o futuro.

I	shall/will	go	eu irei, etc.
you he she it	will		
we	shall/will		
you they	will		

Forma-se o **futuro** com **shall/will + infinito** sem **to**. Na 1.ª pessoa do singular e do plural está a usar-se cada vez mais *will* em vez de *shall*.

2. O Present Tense em vez do Future

> Karl **comes** tomorrow
> Next week he **goes** to the Tate Gallery.

Se a relação com o futuro se faz por meio de advérbios como *tonight*, *tomorrow*, *next week*, etc., podemos empregar o Present Tense em vez do Future.

3. Intenção ou futuro próximo

> a) What **are we going** to see?
> b) We **are going** to visit the Houses of Parliament.
> c) Karl **is leaving** tomorrow.

Para designar uma intenção ou uma acção num futuro próximo, usa-se a expressão **to be going to** *a)*, *b)* ou a **forma progressiva** no presente (c, vd. 13B2).

4. O Future-in-the-Past (Condicional)

> a) I **think** he **will** never **be** at a loss.
> b) Mr. Brown **promised** Karl he **would have** other opportunities later.
> c) Jane **told** Karl she **would take** him to some galleries.

Em algumas frases, o verbo da oração subordinada, referido ao futuro, depende do verbo da oração subordinante. Se o verbo desta estiver no *Present Tense* o verbo dependente fica no *Future*.
Mas se o verbo da subordinante estiver no *Past Tense*, o verbo dependente fica no *Future-in-the-Past*.

I, we	should/would	go	eu iria,
you he she it they	would		etc.

Os verbos da oração subordinante podem ser, por ex.: *to say*, *to tell*, *to believe*, ([bi'li:v] *julgar*), *to hope*, *to think*, *to imagine* ([i'mædʒin] imaginar).

5. O Future II (Futuro composto)

> Next week I **shall have left** London.
> Karl **will have learnt** a lot after his visit to England.

O Futuro composto (*Future II*) serve para expressar uma acção que terminará num determinado ponto do futuro.

I	shall	have left	eu terei partido
you he she it	will		
we	shall		
you they	will		

6. Preposições

> Jane went **from** the station **to** her house.
> John has to work **from** 9 a.m. **to** 5 p.m.
> He got a letter **from** his friend.
> **To** my surprise she was not there.
> [sə'praiz] surpresa

from: l.: de
      t.: a partir de
      c.: de
to l.: para, a, etc.
      t.: até
      c.: para, etc.

the train from London to Bristol	o comboio de Londres para Bristol
he is from Kent	ele é de Kent
from bad to worse	de mal a pior
from now	a partir de agora
to the minute	ao minuto exacto
to go to school	ir para a escola
here's to you	à sua saúde!

> He worked **till** 7 o'clock.
> Mr. Holdstock goes up the Thames **as far as** Windsor.

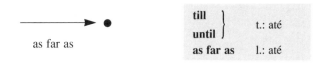

| till / until | t.: até |
| as far as | l.: até |

till now — até agora
not till yesterday — só ontem

7. Verbos fortes e fracos irregulares

to read [iː]	**read** [e]	**read** [e]	ler
to be [i(ː)]	**was** [wɔz, wəz], **were** [wə(ː)]	**been** [i(ː)]	ser, estar
to speak [iː]	**spoke** [əu]	**spoken** [əu]	falar

Exercícios 12 C

1. Escolha dez verbos do texto e forme com eles o Future, o Future-in-the-Past e o Future II, em todas as pessoas.

2. Construa frases que dependam de *say*, *tell*, *hope* e *believe*.
   Use nas mesmas o Present Tense e o Past Tense.

3. Tell a friend:
   a) what you are going to do next week,
   b) what you will do when you are in London,
   c) what you would do if you had much money and time.

4. Traduza: O que vai ele fazer quando chegar? Gostaria de passear connosco? Hoje à noite o Karl vai estar cansado. Ontem a Jane disse-me que ia hoje à City. Amanhã vamos visitar as Casas do Parlamento.

A Road Accident

Texto **13 A**

When Mr. Brown and Karl returned from their tour of the City they found Mrs. Brown rather upset.
«What's wrong?» Mr. Brown asked.
«Well», his wife answered, «as I was walking down Wood Green High Street this morning I saw a terrible accident.»
«Tell us about it, dear», Mr. Brown said.
«Going down the street», Mrs. Brown began, «a car came dashing past me at a tremendous speed. The driver seemed quite reckless, to say the least, for he completely ignored the traffic lights. Then just as he went round the corner a bus came along at right angles, and by the side of the bus, our neighbour's young boy Tom, was riding his bicycle. All three of them met at the corner. The driver of the car put his brakes on so hard that his car skidded and knocked Tom down.»
«Poor boy!» exclaimed Jane, who had come into the room while her mother was talking. «Was he hurt?»
«His right ankle was broken», Mrs. Brown answered, «and he lay there in the street, his face white with pain.»
«And what about the bus?» Jane wanted to know.
«The bus had swerved to the left so that its front wheels mounted the kerb.»
«Was anyone else hurt?»
«An old man standing on the kerb was hit by one of the wheels and badly frightened.»
«Was there a policeman near?» Karl asked.
«The people were crowding round», Mrs. Brown said, «when a policeman appeared. He asked the driver of the car for his licence, and while he was writing the details of the accident in his notebook the man was searching his pockets. But finally the man had to confess that he had no licence.»
«That's bad», Mr. Brown remarked. «It makes the offence worse.»
His wife agreed. «Yes, I think he'll have to pay a very heavy fine when his case comes up before the court. There were many witnesses besides me who saw how it happened.»
«What did they do with poor Tom?» Jane interrupted.

«An ambulance came and took him to the nearest hospital.»
«These road accidents are terrible», Mr. Brown said.
«Some drivers are much too careless.»
«Yes», answered Mrs. Brown. «I'm thankful that our John is a careful driver.»

Notas gramaticais 13 B

1. O Particípio Presente

> A car came **dashing** past me.

O **particípio presente** (*Present Participle*) forma-se juntando **-ing** ao infinito (sem *to*).
São de considerar as seguintes particularidades gráficas:

> to com**e** – coming
> to si**t** – sitting
> to l**ie** – lying

Ao juntar *-ing*:
omite-se o *-e* mudo final,
dobra-se a consoante final precedida de uma só vogal,
o *-ie* final passa a *-y*.
(Vd. as particularidades gráficas relativas aos graus dos adjectivos, 5B3 e ao pretérito, 9B4.)

2. A forma progressiva

> Tom **was riding** his bicycle.

A **forma progressiva** (*Progressive Form* [prə'gresiv fɔːm]) é construída com uma **forma de to be** + o **particípio presente**.

As formas progressivas dos diferentes tempos são:
Presente — **I am riding**
Pretérito — **I was riding**
Pretérito composto — **I have been riding**
Pretérito mais que perfeito — **I had been riding**
Futuro (Condicional) — **I shall (should) be riding**
Futuro (Condicional) composto — **I shall (should) have been riding**

3. Emprego da forma progressiva

> I **was walking** down High Street.

A forma progressiva expressa um processo a decorrer num determinado momento e que continua. Representa o processo no seu decurso.

> The people **were crowding** round, when a policeman appeared.

Expressa também um processo que está a decorrer quando surge um segundo.

> While the policeman **was writing** the details in his notebook the man **was searching** his pockets.

Expressa ainda processos que decorrem simultaneamente.

4. Excepções no emprego da forma progressiva

> I always **get up** at seven o'clock.
> London **lies** on the Thames
> We **hope** for better times.

Não se emprega a forma progressiva:
    em acções que se repetem continuamente,
    em estados de duração limitada.

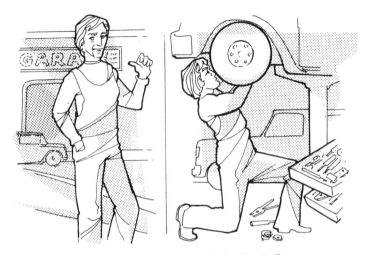

John is a mechanic.
He **works** at a garage.

Is is already 7 p.m.
and he **is** still **working**.

Os verbos cujo significado implica já uma duração só excepcionalmente aparecem na forma progressiva. São entre outros: *to know* (saber), *to hope* (esperar, ter esperança), *to feel* ([fiːl] sentir), *to fear* ([fiə] recear), *to seem* (parecer), *to understand* (compreender), *to like* (gostar), *to love* ([lʌv] amar), *to belong to* ([biˈlɔŋ] pertencer), *to possess* ([pəˈzes] possuir), *to consist of* ([kənˈsist] constar de).
(Vd. emprego do Present Tense, 11B2.)

5. Particularidades da formação do plural

a)						
man	[mæn]	–	men	[men]	homem
woman	[ˈwumən]	–	women	[ˈwimin]	mulher
mouse	[maus]	–	mice	[mais]	rato
goose	[guːs]	–	geese	[giːs]	ganso
foot	[fut]	–	feet	[fiːt]	pé
tooth	[tuːθ]	–	teeth	[tiːθ]	dente

Uma série de substantivos forma o plural por alteração da vogal do radical.

b) Englishman ['iŋgliʃmən] – Englishmen [-mən]   inglês
Frenchman ['frentʃmən] – Frenchmen [-mən]   francês
German ['dʒəːmen] – Germans ['dʒəːmənz]   alemão
Roman ['rəumən] – Romans ['rəumənz]   romano

Os compostos de -*man* formam o plural em -*men*. *German* e *Roman* não são compostos de -*man* e por isso seguem a regra geral para o plural.

6. Preposições

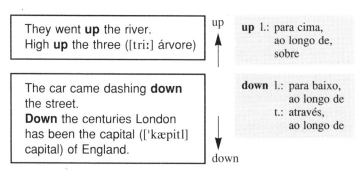

They went **up** the river.
High **up** the three ([triː] árvore)

up 1.: para cima, ao longo de, sobre

The car came dashing **down** the street.
Down the centuries London has been the capital (['kæpitl] capital) of England.

down 1.: para baixo, ao longo de
t.: através, ao longo de

7. Verbos fortes e fracos irregulares

to send	[e]	sent	[e]	sent	[e]	enviar
to buy	[ai]	bought	[ɔː]	bought	[ɔː]	comprar
to tell	[e]	told	[əu]	told	[əu]	contar, narrar
to put	[u]	put	[u]	put	[u]	colocar

Exercícios 13 C

1. Forme o Present Participle dos seguintes infinitos: *to take* [teik] agarrar, *to hope* [həup] esperar, ter esperança, *to smile* [smail] sorrir, *to ride* [raid] montar, *to put* [put] colocar, *to shut* [ʃʌt] fechar, *to hop* [hɔp] saltar, *to die* [dai] morrer, *to play* [plei] brincar, jogar, *to cry* [krai] chorar.
2. Escreva cinco respostas para cada uma das seguintes perguntas:
   a) What were you doing when the accident happened?
   b) What was your father doing, while you were working?

3. Empregue os verbos entre parêntesis nas seguintes frases. Utilize, se possível, a forma progressiva:

London __ on the Thames. (to lie)
Poor Tom __ in the street, until the ambulance arrived. (to lie)
A crowd of people __ around the place where the accident had happened. (to stand)
John __ to work every morning. (to go)
I __ he will have to pay a heavy fine. (to think)

Theatre and Cinema

Texto **14 A**

One evening Jane and Karl talked about going to the theatre and the cinema.

«Where do you like to sit when you go to the cinema?» Karl began.

«Mostly in the stalls, and not too near the screen» replied Jane, «but sometimes in the balcony. Which do you prefer?»

«I'm afraid I don't know the expressions 'stalls' and 'balcony'. Can you explain them to me?»

«Yes, the 'stalls' are the seats on the ground floor. But in larger cinemas there may also be an upper part called a 'balcony' or 'circle'.»

«And how about seats in the theatre? Do you use the same names for those?»

«Yes, partly. But a large theatre may have other names too. On the ground in front you find stalls as in the cinema but the seats behind the stalls, the less expensive ones, are known as 'the pit'. And there may be two balconies, the first called the 'dress circle' and the one above it the 'upper circle'. And above that there may be a 'gallery', for which the slang name is 'the gods'. The cheapest seats you can get in a theatre are in 'the gods'. The most expensive ones are in the boxes or the very front rows of the stalls.»

«You know, Jane», said Karl, «I'd like to take you to the theatre tonight. May I?»

«Thank you very much, Karl», replied Jane, «but I think it might be difficult for us to get tickets at such short notice. For the theatre it's best to book seats beforehand, whereas for the cinema we can usually get tickets at the box-office just before we go in. Frankly I think it would be better to go to the cinema tonight.»
«All right, but don't you really prefer the theatre to the cinema?»
«Yes, I do. I find a live play on the stage much more impressive than any film. A film can't give you the same sense of contact with the actors and actresses. But my brother John doesn't agree. He says the scope of a film is so much wider. It can go anywhere, it can change the scene quickly, give you close-ups as well as long shots, and generally be more realistic. Then too he likes to be able to smoke and you aren't allowed to smoke in many theatres.»
«I see. Well, I agree with him that the cinema has its own advantages over the theatre. I suppose really we shouldn't try to compare them but just to understand them separately as two different forms of art.»
«Yes, that's it. And in any case, if you want to take me to the cinema tonight we had better stop this discussion and decide where to go. May I have a look at that evening paper, please? It has a list of all the films now showing, on one of the inside pages.»

Notas gramaticais   14 B

1. Os verbos defectivos

Os verbos defectivos **can**, **may**, **must**, **will**, **shall**, **need**, **ought to**, **used to**, têm as seguintes particularidades:

a) não têm infinito nem particípio,

b) não têm tempos compostos, para o que precisam de formas supletivas (vd. tb. 10B3).

c)
> He may smoke. — He like**s** the film.

Não tomam *-s* na 3.ª pessoa do singular do presente.

d)
> Where can we go? — Where **do** we go?
> He cannot write. — He **does** not write.

Na interrogativa e na negativa com *not* (*-n't*) não se usa o auxiliar *to do*, ao contrário do que acontece com os outros verbos (vd. 16B1-5).

e)
> I will come. — I want **to** come.

São seguidos de infinito sem *to*, à excepção de *ought to* e *used to*.

f)
> He **can speak** English. = Ele sabe (falar) inglês

São sempre seguidos de outro verbo no infinito (a não ser que este possa ser subentendido).

2. can – could

> I **can** carry the bag.
> He **could** explain it to me.
> We **can** buy the tickets at the box-office.
> You **can** come in.

Can e **could** exprimem capacidade física e psíquica, possibilidade e permissão.

> I **am able to** find my way.
> **It is possible to** buy the tickets at the box-office.

As formas supletivas para **can** são **to be able to** (poder, ser capaz) e **it is possible to/that** (é possível.../que).

> He **cannot** write.
> He **is unable to** write.
> He **is not able to** write the letter now.

A **negativa** de *can* é **cannot** (uma só palavra), a de *to be able to* é **to be unable to** ou **not to be able to**.

3. may – might

> He **may** come tomorrow.
> We **may** smoke here.
> **May** he return soon!

May exprime a possibilidade (talvez), a permissão e o desejo.

> He **cannot** come tomorrow.
> We **may not** smoke here.
> You **must not** smoke here.
> **May** he **never** have an accident!

A possibilidade é negada com **cannot**, a permissão com **may not** (forma reservada) ou **must not** (forma proibitiva), o desejo com **may + negativa** (**not**, **never**, etc.).

> You **might** not like this film. (Talvez..., Possivelmente..., Pode ser que...)
> He bought an expensive ticket, so that he **might** see better.
> He **was allowed to** smoke.

Na oração principal **might** é usado apenas para exprimir uma possibilidade e tem um sentido de dúvida mais forte do que **may**. **Might** só tem significado de passado em orações subordinadas. A permissão no passado, na oração principal, tem de ser usada como um verbo supletivo.

> I **was allowed to** leave earlier.
> You **are permitted to** smoke in the cinema.
> **It is possible that** he will be here soon.

As **formas supletivas** para **may** são **to be allowed to**, **to be permitted to** ([pə'mitid] ter licença de) e **it is possible that** (é possível que).

4. must

> You **must** go now.
> It is eight o'clock, we **have to** go now.
> I **had to** pay for it.

Must exprime uma necessidade ou um dever, que o sujeito pronuncia. Se as circunstâncias não o permitirem usa-se a forma supletiva **to have to**. Uma obrigação no passado também é expressa por uma forma supletiva. (Só em orações subordinadas pode usar-se *must* com significado passado [vd. *might*].)

> He **need not** write this letter now.
> You **must** not go into this room.

A **negativa** para **must** é **need not** (não precisa[s] de) ou **must not** (não pode[s], vd. *may*).

São **formas supletivas** para **must**, **to be obliged to** ([ə'blaidʒd] ser obrigado a), **to be forced to** ([fɔːst]), **to be compelled to** ([kəm'peld] ser forçado a).

5. Preposições

> John lives **with** his parents.
> Tea **with** milk and sugar.
> Jane does her work **with** care.
> ([kɛə] cuidado)
> He was white **with** pain.

with l.: com, junto de
c.: de, com

> You cannot buy anything **without** money.

without c.: sem

> Some famous (['feiməs] célebres)
> buildings lie **within** the city.
> He will phone you **within** an hour.
> He has to live **within** his income.
> (['inkʌm] rendimento)

within
×

within: dentro de

6. Verbos fortes e fracos irregulares

Fixe os seguintes verbos irregulares e forme frases em diversos tempos:

to beat [iː]	beat [iː]	beaten [iː]	bater
to grow [əu]	grew [uː]	grown [əu]	crescer, tornar-se
to strike [ai]	struck [ʌ]	struck [ʌ]	bater
to dream [iː]	dreamt [e]	dreamt [e]	sonhar
também regular	dreamed [iː]	dreamed [iː]	

Exercícios 14 C

1. Procure no texto todos os verbos defectivos e verifique em que acepção estão empregados.
   Construa para cada acepção uma frase semelhante, por ex.: What can we do tonight? (Possibilidade)
   What can you tell me about this film?
2. Escreva os diferentes tempos de *can*, *may*, *must* na 3.ª pessoa do singular e empregue-os numa frase, por ex.: he can, he could, he will be able to, etc. He will be able to read English soon.
3. Do you prefer the live theatre or the cinema? Give your reasons. (reason ['riːzn] razão)

Visiting the Houses of Parliament

Texto **15 A**

«Well Karl», Mr. Brown said to his German guest, «as it's Saturday morning we could pay a visit to the Houses of Parliament, which are open to the public today.»

«I'd like that very much», Karl answered. «I've always wanted to see them.»

«Let's go then», said Mr. Brown. And they took the underground to Westminster. When they came up to the street they caught sight of a tall tower near the bank of the Thames.

«Is that Big Ben over there?» Karl asked.

«Yes», answered Mr. Brown. «Or rather, that's the Clock Tower of the Houses of Parliament, and Big Ben is the great bell in it.»

They crossed the street and entered the buildings by the public entrance.

«The Houses of Parliament», Mr. Brown said, «are one of the most beautiful and interesting places in London. Everybody who comes to this city should see them.»

They joined some other visitors following a guide and came to the Robing Room, a richly decorated hall with a throne. From here the monarch goes into the House of Lords to open Parliament. In the House of Lords Karl admired the splendid red seats, the stained glass windows, the beautiful galleries, and the throne for the Queen. A cushioned red seat in the middle of the room attracted their attention.

«This is the Woolsack», the guide explained. «The Lord Chancellor, who fulfils the office of Speaker in the House, sits on it.»

«Is it really filled with wool?»

«Yes it is», the guide replied. «Wool has played a very important part in the history of Great Britain. You ought to remember that it was one of the sources of the country's wealth and economic power.»

Through the Peers' Lobby they came into the House of Commons, which was destroyed in an air-raid in 1941 but later rebuilt.

«This is the place», the guide said, «where the laws are made for the British nation. The House of Commons now has about 630 members who are elected by ballot. Though the United

Kingdom is a hereditary monarchy ruled by a sovereign the real government is in the hands of the Cabinet, which is responsible to Parliament. The members of the Cabinet are drawn from the party in power.»

«There are four main parties in Britain now, aren't there?», Karl asked.

«Yes, the Conservatives, the Labour Party, the Social Democrats and the Liberals. But besides them we also have several smaller parties, such as the Scottish Nationalists and the Ulster Unionists.»

«Who is the Chairman of the House?»

«Mr. Speaker. You see his chair there in front of the large table in the middle. The Queen's gilded mace is placed before him as a symbol of power. The Prime Minister and his Cabinet occupy the front bench on the right side of the House, the Opposition leaders sit on the left. The other Members of Parliament, M.P.s as we call them for short occupy the back benches.»

Karl and Mr. Brown ended their tour with the guide in the oldest part of the buildings, Westminster Hall, which dates back to the Middle Ages. The early English parliaments were held here, and it was also the scene of the death-sentence passed on Charles I.

«I hope I shall be able to visit more of these interesting places in London», said Karl when they left the Houses of Parliament.

«I'm sure you will», Mr. Brown replied.

Notas gramaticais **15 B**

1. shall – should, ought to

a)
> We **shall** see interesting places in London.
> If I had time, I **should** visit Westminster Hall.

Na 1.ª pessoa do singular e do plural *shall* e *should* servem para formar o futuro e o condicional respectivamente. (Vd. 12B1, 12B4, 12B5, 15B2 a.)

b)
> You **shall** go there now.
> Everybody **should** visit the Houses of Parliament.
> You **ought to** be more careful.

Shall exprime uma ordem directa e enérgica.
Should exprime um dever moral, que com forma mais acentuada se expressa com *ought to* («tu devias...»).

> **You shall** go now. — I know that **I am to** go.

A **forma supletiva** para **shall** é **to be to**:

2. will – would, used to

a)
> John **will** go to Westminster.
> If he had time, he **would** visit Westminster Hall.

Na 2.ª e 3.ª pessoas do singular e do plural, e cada vez mais também na 1.ª pessoa, *will* e *would* servem para formar o futuro e o condicional. (Vd. 12B1, 12B4, 12B5.)

b)
> You can, if you **will**.

Will significa querer apenas para uma forte ênfase.

> I **want to** know her name.

As formas supletivas para **will** são:

to want to [wɔnt]	querer
to wish to [wiʃ]	desejar
would like to [laik]	gostaria de
to be going to	tencionar
to intend to [in'tend]	tencionar
to mean to [miːn]	tencionar
to be willing to	estar disposto a

c) > Children **will** play. – As crianças brincam (sempre).
> When he was a child, he **used to** play in the street.
> He **would** walk for hours.

Will e *would* podem expressar uma acção habitual, que se repete, (costumar fazer). No passado, a forma supletiva é *used to*. As acções habituais também podem ser expressas pelo presente simples (vd. 11B2).

3. need, dare

> He **needs** your help. – Ele precisa do teu auxílio.
> He **needn't** go there. – Ele não precisa lá ir.
> He **dare not** ask. ([dɛə] ousar)

Need (precisar) e *dare* (ousar) tanto podem ser auxiliares com verbos independentes.
Se forem usados como auxiliar:
a) não tomam -*s* na 3.ª pessoa do singular do presente,
b) não são seguidos por *to*, antes do infinito que deles depende,
c) formam a interrogativa e a negativa sem *to do* (vd. 16B2a).

4. Preposições

> There is a garden **between** the house and the street.
> He left his office **between** two and three in the afternoon.
> John saw a football match **between** England and Scotland.

between

between: entre (dois)

> We saw Jane **among** the crowd.
> They quarrelled (to quarrel [ˈkwɔrəl] discutir) **among** themselves.

 among **among:** entre (vários)

5. Verbos fortes e fracos irregulares

to become	[ʌ]	became	[ei]	become	[ʌ]	tornar-se, ficar
to hang	[æ]	hung	[ʌ]	hung	[ʌ]	pendurar
to swim	[i]	swam	[æ]	swum	[ʌ]	nadar
to feed	[iː]	fed	[e]	fed	[e]	alimentar
to build	[i]	built	[i]	built	[i]	construir

Exercícios **15 C**

1. Passe para os diferentes tempos:
   John is to go now. (John was to go then, etc.)
   We are to visit Mr. Brown.
   I am going to write a letter.
   They are willing to help us.

2. Passe as seguintes frases para o Past Tense, Future e Past Perfect, utilizando as formas supletivas correspondentes:
   You shall go there. (agora mesmo)
   We will start on our jorney. (agora mesmo)
   I will tell you about the House of Commons.

3. Mencione acções habituais no passado (used to) e comece as frases com:

   When I was a child...
   When Karl was in London...
   When John went to school...
   When Jane was a little girl...

4. Complete as frases do exercício 3 com o correspondente inglês a:
   a) eu tive que
   b) ele pôde
   c) ele devia
   d) ela não precisava

Fleet Street and Its Newspapers

Texto 16 A

«What have you been doing today, Karl?» asked Mr. Brown one evening when his guest returned home.

Karl smiled. «London again», he said. «After my classes at the language school I walked from Piccadilly Circus to St. Paul's.»

«Then you certainly went through Fleet Street. Did you see the big newspaper offices round there?»

«Well, I saw some of them. I noticed especially the Daily Express building because of its black glass front. And the Daily Telegraph building is close by.»

«That's right. The Daily Mirror building is further away, in High Holborn, and the new Times offices are further away still, in Gray's Inn Road. But Fleet Street is still the centre of London's journalistic world. Nearly all our leading papers and periodicals are published in the area.»

«Do you subscribe to your newspapers and have them delivered by post?» «No, we either get our papers from a newsagent, who is usually a stationer as well, or we buy them in the street.»

«Yes», said Karl. «I've noticed the newspaper-sellers at the street corners. There seem to be a lot of them. Someone once told me you read more newspapers here than in any other country.»

«Well, I'm not sure whether that's still so. But we do read a great many. I expect you've noticed too that nearly all the people travelling on the underground to and from the City carry a newspaper. They take one with them to work in the morning, and usually buy another one, an evening paper, on the way home.»

«Then some of your papers must have a big circulation?»

«Yes, the popular ones do. The Daily Mirror prints more than four million copies a day, the Daily Express more than three million, and there are several more selling one or two million. But our most serious papers, the Times and the Guardian, don't rise far above three hundred thousand copies.»

«Do you like to read more than one paper, Mr. Brown?»

«Yes, I like to have full information on what's happening inside and outside the country, and to read different opinions about it.

"I like the Times especially, because of its wide foreign news service and the fine correspondents it has, stationed all over the world."

THE TIMES

Mrs Thatcher defines new mood for Tory politics

Recession may be levelling out
—Mr Wilson

Summit of six industrial nations next month to examine prospects of economic recovery

Faith in base of capitalism and freedom

Sinai pact gets final approval by Congress

Reshuffle of Spanish military leadership

New set of demands by gang who kidnapped Dutch businessman

Formula may prevent press freedom clash

"I expect you like to read the Times leading articles."
"I do, the paper is famous for them, and they've often exercised great influence on government policy. The business part of the Times is important, too, for anyone interested in finance, commerce or industry. And there are, of course, the correspondence columns."
«The letters to the Editor?»
"Yes, they could well be called a national institution. They come from leading people in all walks of life."
"I know. I've sometimes tried to read them myself. But they're usually too long and difficult for me. Who in the world has the time to study such long letters?"
Mr. Brown laughed. "Well, have a look at the letters in this evening paper then. They're easier!"

Notas gramaticais **16 B**

1. O emprego de «to do»

> **Do** you **know** this paper?
> I **do not** (**don't** [dəunt]) **know** it.
> You really **do not** (**don't** [dəunt]) **know** the Times?

Forma-se a **interrogativa** e a **negativa com** «not» com o verbo *to do* e o infinito do verbo em questão, sem *to*.

Afirmativa	*Interrogativa*	*Negativa com «not»*
He **goes**	**Does** he go?	He **does not** (**doesn't** ['dʌznt]) go.
He **went**	**Did** he go?	He **did not** (**didn't** ['didnt]) go.

2. Excepções no emprego de «to do»

a)
> **Is** that so?
> What **have** you been doing today?
> You **cannot** (**can't** [kɑːnt]) subscribe to newspapers and have them delivered by post.

As frases cujo predicado contém um **verbo auxiliar** (*to be, to have, shall, will, can, may, must, ought to, used to*) não formam a interrogativa nem a negativa com *to do*.
Por conseguinte, *to do* só se emprega nos tempos simples (*Present Tense, Past Tense*), visto que todos os outros tempos se formam com auxiliares.

b)
> **Who** reads The Times?
> **Which of you** knows this leading article?
> **Whose leading articles** exercise an important influence on policy?
> **What** makes you read so many papers?
> (to make = fazer com que)
> **What papers** attract your attention?

As **frases interrogativas** cujo **sujeito** é um pronome interrogativo não se constroem com *to do*.

> Who does **not** (doesn't) read The Times?
> Which of you does **not** (doesn't) know this leading article?
> What papers do **not** (don't) attract your attention?

As interrogativas negativas com **not** formam-se com *to do* quando o sujeito é ou contém um pronome interrogativo.

c) > He knows **nothing** about English papers. (nothing [ˈnʌθiŋ] nada)
> He **never** reads The Times.

Só as frases negativas com *not* se formam com *to do*; as outras negativas não o requerem.

3. O Imperativo na forma negativa

> Don't **be** home late.
> Don't always **be** in a hurry.

O imperativo na negativa forma-se sempre com *to do*, mesmo para verbos auxiliares.

4. Particularidades do verbo «to have» em british english

> **Has** Mr. Brown any German newspapers?
> Mr. Brown **has** no German papers.
> **Does** John **have** lunch at twelve o'clock?
> John **does** not (doesn't) **have** lunch at twelve o'clock.

Se o verbo *to have* for auxiliar de tempos compostos, não forma a interrogativa nem a negativa com *to do*.
Como verbo principal, com o significado de «ter», «possuir» também não forma a interrogativa nem a negativa com *to do*. Mas se significar «tomar», «comer», a interrogativa e a negativa com *not* formam-se com *to do*.

5. «to do» como enfático

> Why did you never read English papers? **Do** read them now. – But I **did** read them.

Em frases afirmativas o emprego do *to do* serve para ênfase. («Lê-os *pelo menos* agora» – «Mas *é que* já os li.»)

6. Preposições

> The Thames makes a bend **above** Oxford.
> (bend [bend] curva)
> The English of some newspapers **is above** me.

above: acima de
por cima de

above all — primeiro que tudo
it is above me — isso ultrapassa-me
he is above me — ele está acima de mim

> In London there are several bridges **over** the Thames.
> We shall be in their house **over** the weekend.
> Mr. Holdstock is **over** me in the office.

over: por cima de
sobre

all over the country — em todo o país
over there — ali do outro lado
over a cup of tea — enquanto se toma uma chávena de chá

7. Verbos fortes e fracos irregulares

to hide	[ai]	hid	[i]	hidden	[i]	esconder
to swing	[i]	swung	[ʌ]	swung	[ʌ]	agitar, balançar
to feel	[iː]	felt	[e]	felt	[e]	sentir
to seek	[iː]	sought	[ɔː]	sought	[ɔː]	procurar

Exercícios **16 C**

1. Explique a razão pela qual *to do* foi empregado ou não nas seguintes frases:

    He speaks English.
    Does he speak English?
    Does he not (Doesn't he) speak English?

    Can he speak English?
    He cannot (can't) speak English.
    Can he not (Can't he) speak English?

    Who speaks English?
    Which of you speaks English?

    Do learn to speak English   (to learn [ləːn], learnt,
    I did learn to speak English.   learnt [ləːnt] aprender)

2. Transforme as seguintes frases de acordo com o exemplo do exercício n.º 1.
    I visit London.
    You walked through the streets.
    He goes by underground.
    She bought «The Times».
    We have breakfast at eight.

3. Escreva as seguintes frases na forma negativa:
    I walked from Piccadilly to Fleet Street. In Fleet Street I noticed the big newspaper houses. The black glass front of the building of the Daily Express attracted my attention.
    Mr. Brown gets his paper from the newsagent. The newsagent is a stationer. He has his shop in Wood Green. Mr. Brown likes the Times very much. He always reads the leading articles.

4. Recapitule os pronomes e advérbios interrogativos (4B1-4) e faça perguntas cuja resposta seja a parte em itálico das seguintes frases:
    Exemplo: *When John and Karl came up*, they caught sight of a tall tower.
    Pergunta: When did John and Karl catch sight of a tall tower?

The clock tower of the House of Parliament is called «Big Ben».
The Victoria [vikˈtɔːriə] *Tower* is the tallest tower of the Houses of Parliament.
Everybody should see *the Houses of Parliament*.
In the House of Lords *Karl* admired the stained glass windows.
They joined *some other visitors.*
A *cushioned red seat* attracted Karl's attention.
The Woolsack is *the Lord Chancellor's* seat.
Wool has played a very important part in the history of Great Britain.
In the House of Commons the laws are made for the British people.
The House of Commons has *about* 630 members.
The real government is in the hands *of the Cabinet.*
The members of the Cabinet are drawn from the *leading* party.
The Speaker's chair is in front of the large table in the middle.
The Queen's gilded mace is placed *before him.*
The Prime Minister and his Cabinet sit on the *ritht* side of the House.

5. Do mesmo modo, faça perguntas que tenham como resposta palavras e grupos de palavras do texto da lição n.º 16, à sua escolha.

London Concert Halls

Texto **17 A**

When Karl came home one Friday evening he found Jane waiting for him. «Look, Karl», she said, «I've got some tickets for a concert.»
«Where is it, where are we going?», Karl wanted to know.
«To the Royal Albert Hall. There's going to be a Handel Concert there tomorrow.»
«Who's playing?» Karl asked.
Jane had a look at the programme. «The BBC Symphony Orchestra», she read, «conducted by Rudolf Kempe from Germany. The organ will be played by someone from Germany too, but I'm afraid I can't pronounce *his* name.»
Karl smiled. «So I'm going to hear the music of a German composer played by a German organist!»

«I suppose so, if you think Handel is really a German composer.»
«Why, of course. He was born in Germany, at Halle.»
«But he lived here in England for years and years and most of his works were composed here. Don't forget that he was buried in the Poet's Corner of Westminster Abbey.»
«Well, let's not quarrel about Handel», Karl laughed. «Let's call him a German-English composer and be glad that our two countries have a famous composer in common. But tell me something about the concert hall. Why is it called the Albert Hall?»
«It got its name from Prince Albert, the Consort of Queen Victoria – another German, by the way, who became an Englishman. You can see his monument, the Albert Memorial, in Kensington Gardens – a continuation of Hyde Park. The Albert Hall, a huge circular building, faces it on the other side of Kensington Road. The Hall has room for 8,000 people, I believe and it's used not only for concerts but also for public meetings, boxing matches and even for balls.»
«Are there any other large concert halls in London?» Karl asked.
«Oh yes. I suppose the best known is the Royal Festival Hall by the Thames near Waterloo Bridge. Some very good concerts are given there.»
«Then I must go there too, one day, Jane.»

Notas gramaticais **17 B**

1. A Passiva

> Activa: Someone **asked** John a question.
> Passiva: John **was asked** a question.

Há em inglês – como em português – voz activa e passiva.
Na voz activa o sujeito (*someone*) realiza a acção (*asked*) que incide sobre os complementos (*John, a question*). A voz activa diz que o sujeito pratica a acção.
Na voz passiva o sujeito é *John*. A acção incide sobre ele.
A voz passiva diz que o sujeito sofre a acção.

A língua inglesa tem mais de uma possibilidade de passiva; (normal e idiomática; nesta o complemento indirecto passa para sujeito).
Em geral, emprega-se a passiva quando o locutor pretende pôr em evidência a acção que o predicado expressa.

2. Formação da Passiva

> Handel **was buried** in the Poets' Corner.

A passiva forma-se com «to be» + Past Participle. Os tempos são:

Present Tense:	**it is done** [dʌn] é feito
Past Tense:	**it was done** foi (era) feito
Future I:	**it will be done** será feito
Conditional I:	**it would be done** seria feito
Present Perfect	**it has been done** tem sido (foi) feito
Past Perfect:	**it had been done** tinha sido (fora) feito
Future II:	**it will have been done** terá sido feito
Conditional II:	**it would have been done** teria sido feito

3. Verbos transitivos e intransitivos

> They **helped** Mother.
> Mother **was helped**.

Chamam-se transitivos os verbos que têm complemento directo. Em português, só se forma a passiva com verbos transitivos.

Com os seguintes verbos ingleses pode formar-se uma passiva de sujeito pessoal:

to advise [əd'vaiz]	aconselhar
to allow [ə'lau]	permitir
to approach [ə'prəutʃ]	aproximar-se
to assist [ə'sist]	ajudar
to believe [bi'li:v]	acreditar
to command [kə'mɑ:nd]	ordenar
to follow ['fɔləu]	seguir
to help [help]	ajudar
to join [dʒɔin]	juntar-se a
to meet [mi:t]	encontrar-se com
to obey [ə'bei]	obedecer
to order ['ɔ:də]	ordenar
to permit [pə'mit]	permitir
to remember [ri'membə]	lembrar-se
to serve [sə:v]	servir
to thank [θæŋk]	agradecer
to trust [tʌst]	confiar

4. Passagem da Activa para a Passiva

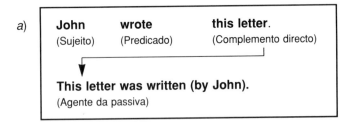

Ao passar uma frase da activa para a passiva, o complemento directo da activa passa para sujeito da passiva.

O agente da passiva é precedido de *by*, mas só é usado quando o sentido da frase o exige; por ex., numa frase como *The BBC Symphony Orchestra is conducted by Rudolf Kempe*. Num caso destes é preferível a activa.

b)
> I gave **her**   **the tickets**.
>   (Complemento)   (Complemento
>   indirecto)   directo)
>
> **She** ◄──── was given the tickets.
> (Sujeito)
>
> **The tickets** were given (to) her.
> (Sujeito)

Tanto o complemento indirecto como o directo de uma activa podem passar a sujeito da passiva.

5. Preposições

> I wrote my name **below** the line. ([lain] linha).
> He sat **below** me at the concert.

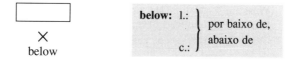

below: l.: ⎫
            ⎬ por baixo de, abaixo de
        c.: ⎭

it is below him   está abaixo da sua dignidade

> We passed **under** Westminster bridge.
> They will answer your letter in **under** three days.
> John's friend is a young man of **under** thirty.

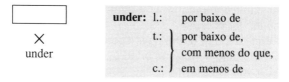

under: l.:   por baixo de
        t.: ⎫ por baixo de,
            ⎬ com menos do que,
        c.: ⎭ em menos de

6. Verbos fortes e fracos irregulares

Leia e recapitule os seguintes verbos irregulares e forme com eles frases em diversos tempos e pessoas:

to bid	[i]	bade	[æ, ei]	bidden	[i]	oferecer, ordenar
to hold	[əu]	held	[e]	held	[e]	segurar
to take	[ei]	took	[u]	taken	[ei]	agarrar, tomar
to have	[æ, ə]	had	[æ, ə]	had	[æ, ə]	ter
to sell	[e]	sold	[əu]	sold	[əu]	vender

Exercícios 17 C

1. Passe para os diferentes tempos:
   You are given the tickets.
   He is asked some questions.
   Tom's right ankle is broken.
   He is helped by his friends.
   The Houses of Parliament are visited by many people.
2. Passe as seguintes frases para a passiva:
   Mr. Brown showed (to show [ʃəu] mostrar) Karl the Houses of Parliament. – He told his guest many interesting things about Westminster Hall. – He gave Karl a book about Charles I. – Mr. Brown promised Karl further trips through London. –
3. Construa mais frases na passiva.

Sport in England

Texto 18 A

Coming down to breakfast one Sunday morning Karl found John reading the newspaper.

«What are you reading?» he asked.

«The sports page.»

«But it's all about cricket.»

«Yes, about yesterday's Test Match.»

«I can't understand why your newspapers reserve so much space for cricket.»

«Well, it's one of the chief sporting interests of English people. So it has to be fully reported by the papers.»

«Do you like playing cricket yourself?»

«Yes, I used to play it at school, and was chosen for the First Eleven. And I belong to the local Cricket Club. I'm considered quite a good player and am often made use of.»
«I should like to see you play.»
«Then I'll take you to our next match. But wouldn't you like to see one of the big matches played at Lord's Cricket Ground in Marylebone, or at the Oval in South London?»
«I don't think so. As a German I'm really more interested in football, you know.»
«Yes, it's a pity you weren't here in the football season. We could have gone to see a match at the Arsenal Ground. Matches there are watched by thousands of people. Or we might have seen a game of rugby.»
«What other sporting events are there besides cricket at this time of year?»
«Well, there are the tennis championships at Wimbledon, and the rowing races at Henley.»
«You mean the Oxford and Cambridge Boat Race?»
«No, that's rowed in London earlier in the year, round about Easter. The races at Hanley are between all kinds of rowing clubs and between individual oarsmen too.»
«What about horse-racing?»
«Yes there's plenty of that. The Derby and the Oaks are run on Epsom Downs in June, and the Ascot race-meetings are famous too. They're usually attended by the Queen. Why are you asking about horse-racing? Do you want to do some betting?»
«Well, I think it would be a plty to go to a race and not place a bet. I should be laughed at!»
«Then you'd better get to know our neighbour opposite. He's a bookmaker!»

Notas gramaticais 18 B

1. A Passiva com verbos ligados a preposição

> They **would laugh at** him.
> He **would be laughed at**.

Com **verbos ligados a preposição**, esta coloca-se na passiva imediatamente **a seguir ao verbo**.

2. A Passiva de verbos com complemento directo e preposição

> They **make use of** him.
> He **is made use of**.

Com determinadas expressões de **verbo + complemento directo + preposição** mantém-se a expressão na passiva. Essas expressões são entre outras:

to find fault with	[faind 'fɔːlt wið]	censurar
to lay hold of	[lei 'həuld əv]	deitar a mão a
to make use of	[meik 'juːs əv]	utilizar
to put an end to	[put ən 'end tə]	pôr fim a
to take care of	[teik 'kɛər əv]	tomar conta de
to take notice of	[teik 'nəutis əv]	notar
to take pity on	[teik 'piti ɔn]	ter piedade de
to take possession of	[teik pə'zeʃən əv]	tomar posse de

3. A Passiva com verbos de ligação

> They called **him** **John**.
> (C. directo) (Nome predicativo do c.d.)
> **He** was called **John**.
> (Sujeito) (Nome predicativo do suj.)
> They consider **John a good player**.
> **He** is considered **a good player**.

Os verbos de ligação (fazer, eleger, nomear) ou (considerar) têm na activa um complemento directo e um nome predicativo do complemento directo. Na passiva corresponde-lhes um sujeito e um nome predicativo do sujeito. São entre outros:

to appoint	[ə'pɔint]	nomear
to call	[kɔːl]	apelidar
to choose	[tʃuːz]	escolher
to consider	[kən'sidə]	considerar
to create	[kri'eit]	criar
to crown	[kraun]	coroar
to declare	[di'klɛə]	declarar
to elect	[i'lektt]	eleger
to make	[meik]	fazer
to proclaim	[prə'kleim]	proclamar

4. Preposições

> Karl went **round** the Albert Hall with Jane.
> This is the most interesting building **around** St. Paul's.
> All the year **round** there are many foreigners in London.

(a)round

(a)round: l.: à volta de
t.: ao longo de

> Karl and John walked **about** the City.
> John's friend is **about** twenty-two.
> John knows all **abou**t cars.

about

about: l.: por
t.: cerca de
c.: acerca de

I have no money about me.   Não trago dinheiro comigo.
Look about you.   Olha à tua volta.
about this time   mais ou menos a esta hora
about £60   cerca de 60 libras

5. Verbos fortes e fracos irregulares

Decore e recapitule os seguintes verbos e construa com eles frases nos diferentes tempos e pessoas:

to know [əu]	**knew** [juː]	**known** [əu]	saber, conhecer
to throw [əu]	**threw** [uː]	**thrown** [əu]	atirar
to send [e]	**sent** [e]	**sent** [e]	enviar

Exercícios 18 C

1. Empregue os diferentes tempos nas seguintes frases:
   Much space is reserved for cricket.

It is reported by the papers.
You are chosen for the First Eleven.
Matches are watched by thousands of people.
The Oxford and Cambridge Boat Race is rowed in London.
The Derby and the Oaks are run at Epsom.
They are attended by the Queen.

2. Construa frases na passiva com as expressões do n.º 2 das NOTAS GRAMATICAIS.
3. Construa frases na passiva com as expressões do n.º 3 das NOTAS GRAMATICAIS.

A Letter to Germany

Texto **19 A**

64, Eastern Avenue,
Wood Green,
Middlesex, England
21st July, 19...

Dear Alfred,

I have been in London for nearly three weeks now and so I had better write the letter I promised to send to you. As you asked I am writing in English and since my host, Mr. Brown, has corrected it, I think the English should be in order.

Mr. Brown told me a saying of Dr. Samuel Johnson, the famous man of letters. He said: «To be tired of London is to be tired of life, for there is in London all that life can afford.» Well, I'm certainly not yet tired of this marvellous city and am still on the go and trying to learn as much as I can about it.

Of course London, besides being the capital, is the centre of commerce and trade for the whole country. The traffic in the streets in the City and around Westminster is tremendous. You see thousands of vehicles and millions of people entering and leaving every day. Everywhere crowds hurrying along the pavement: businessmen, office girls, shoppers and tourists.

The day before yesterday I visited St. Paul's and admired the work of Sir Christopher Wren, the great architec who planned the rebuilding of the heavily-destroyed City after the Great Fire of 1666. I read the memorial inscription to him inside the Cathedral: «If you seek his monument look around you.» And I went up to the famous Whispering Gallery, where even a whisper can be heard on the opposite side of the dome a hundred feet away.

From the Stone Gallery outside the huge dome I had a fine view of London. I saw the streets of the City, packed with offices, banks and warehouses, and the dark, heavy walls of the Tower, beside the bank of the Thames. And after seeing St. Paul's I went on to the Mansion House, which is the Lord Mayor's official residence. The pageant on November 9th, when the Lord Mayor takes office, is one of London's traditional shows.

So Alfred, to sum up: I enjoy being in London and staying with the Brown family. And I like going out with John and Jane in the evening – especially with Jane!

Yours,
Karl.

Notas gramaticais 19 B

1. O Infinito

O Infinito, os Particípios (vd. 9B2, 10B2, 13B1, 21B1-5) e o Gerúndio (vd. 22B1-5, 23B1-2) podem exercer as funções de um substantivo, adjectivo ou pronome. Em inglês usam-se para evitar orações subordinadas.

São as seguintes as formas do Infinito:

simples (activo)	**to ask**	perguntar
forma progressiva	**to be asking**	estar a perguntar
perfeito (activo)	**to have asked**	ter perguntado
simples (passivo)	**to be asked**	ser perguntado
perfeito (passivo)	**to have been asked**	ter sido perguntado

Na frase o Infinito pode ser empregado com ou sem *to*.

2. O Infinito com «to»

> a) **To be tired** of London is **to be tired** of life.
> b) It is very interesting **to visit** St. Paul's. (= To visit St. Paul's is...)
> c) I promised **to write**.
> d) I know how **to go** there.
> e) John was the first **to arrive** and the last **to go**.

O Infinito com *to* pode ter várias posições na frase:

a) O primeiro Infinito desta frase é o sujeito.
   O segundo Infinito é nome predicativo do sujeito. Como tal o Infinito com *to* aparece depois dos verbos *to be*, *to appear*, *to seem*.

b) Depois de expressões impessoais (*it is*, *it appears*, *it seems*) o infinito com *to* é de facto o sujeito (o chamado sujeito «*lógico*»).

c) O Infinito com *to* pode ser complemento directo.

d) Depois de interrogativos, o Infinito com *to* pode ser complemento directo dos verbos *to ask*, *to know*, *to see*, *to tell*.

e) Depois de numerais ordinais, de superlativos e de *the only* (o único), o Infinito com *to*, pode ser atributo.

3. O Infinito sem «to»

> There is in London all that life can **afford**.
> Karl would rather **go** out with Jane.

Emprega-se o Infinito sem *to* depois de:

— verbos defectivos excepto *ought to*, *used to*, (vd. 14B1-4, 15B1-3),
— depois das expressões:

I had better	era melhor eu...
I would rather	eu preferia...
I had best	o melhor seria eu...

4. O Infinito da Passiva

> Every whisper can **be heard** on the opposite side of the dome.
> The inscription is **to be seen** inside the Cathedral.

Se um infinito tiver significado passivo, toma quase sempre a forma passiva. Apesar do significado passivo, usa-se muitas vezes a forma activa do infinito:
- depois de adjectivos quando o sentido da frase não for equívoco (Money is hard to get.).
- depois de *there is*, *there are* (There is nothing to laugh at.).
- com os verbos *to let* (alugar) (This house is to let.) e *to blame* ([bleim] censurar) (He is not to blame.).

5. Expressões idiomáticas com o Infinito

> I am on **the go**.

Em determinadas expressões idiomáticas o Infinito com função de substantivo é precedido pelo artigo. São entre outras:

to have a try [trai]	fazer uma tentativa
to be on the go	estar em movimento
to have a swim [swim]	nadar
to have a drink [driŋk]	tomar uma bebida
to have the lead [liːd]	assumir o comando
to have a look round	olhar em volta

> **To tell the truth**: I do not like it.
> **To sum up**: I am tired of it.

Algumas expressões idiomáticas com o Infinito referem-se ao conteúdo de toda a frase:

to arrive at a conclusion [kənˈkluːʒən]	chegar a uma conclusão
to be open about it	para ser franco
to begin with	para começar, em primeiro lugar
to cut the matter [ˈmætə] short	em poucas palavras
to judge [dʒʌdʒ] from	para ajuizar de...
to sump up [sʌm ˈʌp]	para resumir
to tell the truth [truːθ]	para dizer a verdade

6. Preposições

> They walk **towards** the river.
> He will be back **towards** the end of this week.
> His feelings (['fiːliŋz] sentimentos) **towards** her were friendly.

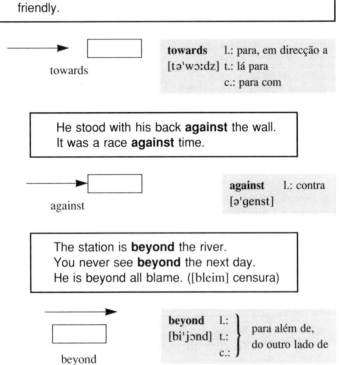

towards

towards l.: para, em direcção a
[tə'wɔːdz] t.: lá para
c.: para com

> He stood with his back **against** the wall.
> It was a race **against** time.

against

against l.: contra
[ə'genst]

> The station is **beyond** the river.
> You never see **beyond** the next day.
> He is beyond all blame. ([bleim] censura)

beyond

beyond l.:
[bi'jɔnd] t.: } para além de,
        c.: do outro lado de

7. Verbos fortes e fracos irregulares

to choose	[uː]	**chose**	[əu]	**chosen**	[əu]	escolher
to lie	[ai]	**lay**	[ei]	**lain**	[ei]	estar (em posição horizontal)
to lay	[ei]	**laid**	[ei]	**laid**	[ei]	pôr
to hit	[i]	**hit**	[i]	**hit**	[i]	atingir
to make	[ei]	**made**	[ei]	**made**	[ei]	fazer

Exercícios 19 C

1. Escreva as diferentes formas do Infinito de: to call, to see, to drive, to take, to visit.
2. Construa frases de acordo com os exemplos do n.º 2 das NOTAS GRAMATICAIS.
3. Construa frases com o Infinito sem «to».
4. Construa frases com o Infinito na passiva.
5. Construa frases com as expressões do n.º 5 das NOTAS GRAMATICAIS.

Dining Out

Texto 20 A

Karl wanted to repay Jane for the evening at the concert. So he decided to ask her to have a meal with him. «I would like you to have dinner with me tonight», he said to her one morning at breakfast.
«That would be lovely», she answered, «where shall we go?»
«Oh, you choose, please. I'm sure you know the possibilities better than I do.»
«Well, what kind of food would you like to have – English, French, Italian, Spanish, Chinese? Or German perhaps? We have restaurants of every nationality in London, and there's a very good German one in Soho, I believe.»
«No thanks,» replied Karl, «German food isn't any change for me, and if you don't mind I'd rather go to a really English place.»
«Then in that case», said Jane, «I suggest we go to the Cheshire Cheese in Fleet Street. That's very English. And it's a very interesting place, too, an old tavern. Our manager, Mr. Morrow, often takes foreign visitors there.»
«It sounds splendid», Karl agreed, «so where shall we meet? I have an English class until half past six.»
«All right, I'll meet you then at the school.»
Punctually at half past six Jane was on the pavement outside the school where Karl had his lessons. She heard a clock strike close by and saw the the school door open as Karl came out. «Hello, Jane», he called, «I didn't expect you to be so punctual! I've telephoned the restaurant to book a table, so we've plenty of time.»

«Then let's walk there», she answered, «it isn't far.»

Karl let Jane lead the way and they walked through Covent Garden, past the Royal Opera House, and into Fleet Street, past the Law Courts.

Beside an old tobacconist's shop they saw a narrow passageway and a sign pointing to the restaurant entrance. As they went in the head waiter asked them, «Have you booked a table?»

«Yes», said Karl, «a table for two in the name of Schmidt. But we're a little early, I think.»

«Then I'm afraid I must ask you to wait. But if you would like to have a drink first in the bar opposite, I'll call you as soon as the table is ready.»

They crossed to the bar, where Jane had a gin and tonic and Karl some of the draught beer for which the house is well known. Then the head waiter called them back and showed them to a wooden seat in the corner. On the wall above the seat was a portrait of Dr. Johnson, who used to live nearby and often came to dine at «The Cheese».

Karl and Jane sat down and looked at the menu. «What would you like to order, sir?» asked the waiter.

«What can you recommend?»

«Well, our speciality here is the famous steak and kidney pudding, but our roast beef and Yorkshire pudding is also very good.»

«Then I'll have the roast beef and Yorkshire», said Jane. «And I the steak and kidney», added Karl.

«Thank you, sir. And something to start with perhaps?»

Karl looked across at Jane. «Yes, melon for me, please.»

«And soup for me. And please may I have the wine list?»

«Certainly, sir. I'll tell the wine waiter to come to you.»

As they finished the main course the waiter came to their table again. «Would you like anything to follow – a sweet or some cheese, perhaps?»

«What sweets have you?»

«Let me see. We have pancakes, apple tart or fresh strawberries and cream.»

«The strawberries and cream for me, please», exclaimed Jane. «And I'll try the pancakes», said Karl. «Then bring some coffee both of us, and let me have the bill.»

«Thank you, Karl, for a most enjoyable meal», said Jane afterwards when they were ready to go. «Now I know why Mr. Morrow brings his visitors here!»

Notas gramaticais 20 B

1. O Complemento Directo acompanhado de Infinito

> I see **him come**. (= I see that he comes.)
> Eu vejo-o vir.   (= Eu vejo que ele vem.)

É uma construção muito comum em inglês. Note-se que:

o complemento directo da oração subordinante: I see **him.**
é ao mesmo tempo
o sujeito da subordinada: (that) **he** comes.

Este Infinito pode ser empregado na frase com ou sem *to*.

2. O Infinito sem «to»

> She heard **a clock** strike.
> He always **makes us** laugh.
> Let **me have** the bill.

Emprega-se o Infinito sem *to* depois de verbos sensitivos e de *to make* (fazer com que), *to let* (permitir), *to have* (levar a; na negativa: não permitir).

3. O Infinito com «to»

> *a)* Karl wanted **Jane to go** to the cinema with him.
> *b)* Mr. Holdstock told **her to buy** stamps.
> *c)* They thought **John (to be)** a good player.

Emprega-se o Infinito com *to*:

a) depois de verbos volitivos e que expressam sentimentos, por ex. *to wish*, *to want*, *to like*, *to love* ([lʌv] amar), *to prefer*, *to hate* ([heit] detestar), *to intend* ([in'tend] tencionar), *to mean* ([miːn] tencionar);

b) depois de verbos que exprimem motivação e permissão, por ex., *to allow* ([ə'lau] permitir), *to command* ([kə'mɑnd] ordenar), *to expect* ([iks'pekt] esperar, estar na expectativa), *to forbid* ([fə'bid] proibir), *to order* (['ɔːdə] ordenar), *to permit* ([pə'mit] permitir), *to tell* (ordenar);

c) depois de verbos de expressão e de pensamento, em especial na linguagem escrita, ao passo que na linguagem comum se prefere neste caso uma oração subordinada com *that*.

To be pode ser omitido, no caso de a frase não se tornar equívoca. São verbos de expressão e de pensamento: *to believe*, *to declare* ([di'klɛə] declarar), *to deny* ([di'nai] negar), *to expect*, *to find*, *to imagine* ([i'mædʒin] imaginar), *to judge* ([dʒʌdʒ] ajuizar) *to know*, *to prove* ([pruːv] demonstrar), *to report* ([ri'pɔːt] participar), *to think*, *to suppose* ([sə'pəuz] supor), *to understand*. Pelo contrário, depois dos verbos *to say*, *to hope*, *to fear* ([fiə] temer), *to answer*, *to reply* usa-se sempre uma oração com *that*.

4. O Sujeito com o Infinito

> They saw **him enter** the room.
> **He** was seen **to enter** the room.
> They thought **him to be** a good player.
> **He** was thought **to be** a good player.

A passiva correspondente a uma frase de complemento directo com infinito (vd. 17B1-4, 18B1-3) apresenta o sujeito com infinito. Nesta construção da passiva o infinito vai sempre acompanhado de *to*.

> They say **that** the food there is very good.
> **The food** there is said **to be** very good.

Depois de *to say*, embora não seja possível um complemento directo acompanhado de infinito (vd. 20B3c), é frequentemente usada a passiva *it is said to be* (diz-se que é…).

5. Preposições

> In London there are many bridges **across** the Thames.
> Yesterday John came **across** an old friend.

across l.: através
c.: «ao encontro de»

to come across — encontrar, dar com

> Last year Jane travelled **through** Scotland.
> It rained **through** the whole week.
> I heard this news **through** a friend of my father's.

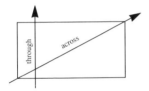

through l.: através
t.: durante
c.: por, com, de

to get through — acabar (trabalho, etc.)
to be through — (telefone) estar ligado
I am through with him — por mim acabei com ele
through fear [fiə] — com medo

6. Verbos fortes e fracos irregulares

to come	[ʌ]	**came**	[ei]	**come**	[ʌ]	vir
to ride	[ai]	**rode**	[əu]	**ridden**	[i]	andar (a cavalo, de bicicleta, etc.)
to wake	[ei]	**woke***	[əu]	**woke(n)***	[əu]	acordar
to hurt	[əː]	**hurt**	[əː]	**hurt**	[əː]	ferir, magoar
to shoot	[uː]	**shot**	[ɔ]	**shot**	[ɔ]	atirar (dar tiros)

* a par da forma fraca **waked.**

Exercícios 20 C

1. Procure nas frases do texto infinitos dependentes do complemento directo e explique o respectivo emprego.
2. Ligue cada conjunto de duas frases com um infinito dependente do complemento directo da primeira:
   Jane saw Karl. He came out of the school door.
   They heard the waiter. He asked them what they wanted to have.
   Karl asks the waiter. He brings the wine list.
   Karl watches Jane. She studies the menu.
3. Forme frases com um infinito dependente de *to make*, *to let*, *to order*.
4. Transforme as seguintes frases utilizando o infinito dependente do complemento directo ou do sujeito:
   Karl thought German food was not any change for him.
   Karl found that the Cheshire Cheese was a very interesting place.
   Karl believed that John was a good mechanic.
   Jane knows that Mr. Holdstock takes foreign visitors there.
5. Forme frases com cada um dos verbos do n.º 3a, b, c, das NOTAS GRAMATICAIS, usando o infinito dependente do complemento directo.
6. Forme 10 frases com ... *is/are said to*...

The BBC Television Centre

Texto 21 A

When he was still in Germany Karl used to listen to the BBC radio programmes, especially the news and the English by Radio lessons, because he wanted to improve his knowledge of the language. Now he is in England he finds watching television helps him with his English too. Mr. Brown explains to him that there are two television services in Britain, the BBC, which draws its funds from licence-fees, and ITV or Independent Television, which is financed by advertising.

«Is it possible to visit any of the television studios?» Karl asked.
«Well, you usually have to wait to go with a party. But a friend of mine, George Hill, happens to work for BBC TV. I'll ask him if he can help.»

Mr. Hill could, and so, on the appointed day, Karl went to Shepherd's Bush and though he didn't know this part of London

very well he soon found his way to the BBC Televisio
at White City. Approaching the Centre he saw a huge
circular in shape, with an open court in the middle.

Karl went in by the entrance-hall. Many people were coming and going. He asked a receptionist for Mr. Hill, who soon came to show him round. And while Mr. Hill told him how the programmes were prepared Karl followed him through the different parts of the building. The studios from which broadcasting takes place are all constructed inside the building so that outside sounds can be kept out. As they have no windows they are lit by artificial light and have to be supplied with fresh air through ventilators. Having seen the television news studios, they went along a corridor and came to the music studios.

«Of course, our programmes can't all be done from here», Mr. Hill said. «Very often, cameras and microphones have to be put in places outside the studios. The signals are then passed to us to be broadcast from the transmitters.»

Finally they had a look into the studios used for the production of television plays and light entertainment programmes. Karl was impressed by their size and by all the scenery and the studio arc-lights and equipament.

«And remember», said Mr. Hill, «that we also make and keep a great many programmes on film. So we have a very large film library.»

Before leaving the building Karl thanked Mr. Hill for his kindness. «I shall understand the working of the programmes much better now», he said. And, the evening coming on, he made his way back to Wood Green.

Notas gramaticais   21 B

1. O Particípio

Há em inglês
um Particípio Presente (Present Participle): ask**ing**
                                               perguntando
e um Particípio Passado (Past Participle): ask**ed**
                                               perguntado.

(Para a construção destas formas vd. 10B2, 13B1; para a pronúncia e grafia 9B3 e 4.)

O Particípio está entre verbo e adjectivo. Deriva de um verbo e, como tal, desenvolve formas para os tempos principais na activa e na passiva:

	Activa	Passiva
Presente	**asking**	**being asked**
Passado	**having asked**	**having been asked**

Por outro lado é usado como adjectivo para qualificar um substantivo:
   The book is **interesting**.   (Nome predicativo do sujeito)
      An **interesting** book.   (Atributo)

2. O Particípio como Atributo

> The BBC Television Centre is a Highly **interesting** place.
> On the **appointed** day Karl went to Shepherd's Bush.
> They had a look into the studios **used** for the production of television plays.

O particípio presente/passado pode servir para qualificar um substantivo – como um adjectivo. Em geral precede o substantivo; mas segue-o se for mais fortemente acentuado ou ligado a uma expressão.

3. O Particípio como parte do Predicado

> Many people were **coming** and **going**.
> Karl sat in the entrance-hall **waiting** for Mr. Hill.
> The studios are **lit** by artificial light.
> Karl was **impressed** by the scenery and equipment.
> Karl looked **surprised**.

O particípio presente aparece como parte do predicado na forma progressiva (vd. 13B2-4) e depois de verbos de repouso e movimento, por ex., *to sit, to stand, to lie, to go, to come, to leave, to remain*.
O particípio passado é parte do predicado na passiva (vd. 17B1 e 2, 18B1-3) e depois de certos verbos intransitivos.

4. O Particípio ligado e independente

a)
> **Having watched** BBC television very often, Karl had improved his knowledge of English.
> **Before leaving** the building, Karl thanked Mr. Hill for his kindness.
> A friend of Mr. Brown's **working** for BBC television, had shown Karl round the studios.

Nas duas primeiras frases o particípio aparece em vez de orações subordinadas («Como o Karl via a BBC muitas vezes…»); («Antes de o Karl sair do edifício…»). O particípio pode ser ligado à oração subordinante com ou sem conjunção – isto se a frase não resultar confusa. As conjunções *if* (se), *unless* ([ən'les] a não ser que) e *though* ([ðəu] embora) não podem ser omitidas.

Na terceira frase o particípio equivale a uma oração relativa («Um amigo do Sr. Brown que trabalha para…»).

Nas três frases a oração subordinante e o particípio estão ligados por um sujeito comum, daí a designação «particípio ligado».

b)
> The evening **coming on**, Karl went back to Wood Green.

Aqui a oração subordinante e o particípio têm cada um o seu sujeito (*Karl* e *evening*); daí a designação de particípio independente, que quase só aparece na linguagem escrita.

5. O Particípio e o Infinito dependentes de Verbos Sensitivos

> I saw Karl **go** to Piccadilly Circus.
> I saw Karl **going** down Oxford Street.

Depois de verbos sensitivos pode usar-se o particípio presente em vez do infinito sem *to* (vd. 20B1 e 2). Ao passo que o Infinito refere o facto em si («Eu vi o Karl ir para Piccadilly Circus.»), o particípio designa o decurso da acção («Eu vi-o a seguir ao longo da Oxford Street.»).

6. Preposições

> They stood **before** the National Gallery.
> The day **before** yesterday we visited the House of Parliament.
> An interesting time lies **before** us.

× before

before l.: em frente de
t.: antes de
c.: antes de, de, com

before long	em breve
before now	já antes
to be before one's time	estar adiantado
the month before last	no penúltimo mês
the day before yesterday	anteontem

> A clerk was standing **behind** the counter.
> The bus was **behind** time.
> There is something **behind** his words.

× behind

behind l.: atrás de
t.: depois de
c.: depois de

to be behind time	estar atrasado
what is behind all this?	o que há por detrás disso?

> Karl came **after** John.
> **After** some time he had learnt English well.
> John is called **after** his father.

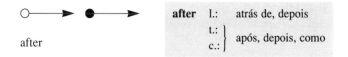

after

after	l.:	atrás de, depois
	t.:	após, depois, como
	c.:	

day after day — dia após dia
time after time — constantemente
the day after tomorrow — depois de amanhã
the month after next — daqui a dois meses
after all — afinal

7. Verbos fortes e fracos irregulares

to do	[du(ː)]	did	[i]	done	[ʌ]	fazer
to ring	[i]	rang	[æ]	rung	[ʌ]	tocar (campainha)
to wear	[ɛə]	wore	[ɔː]	worn	[ɔː]	usar (roupa)
to keep	[iː]	kept	[e]	kept	[e]	guardar, conservar
to show	[əu]	showed	[əu]	shown	[əu]	mostrar

Exercícios 21 C

1. Escreva as diferentes formas do particípio de: *to call*, *to see*, *to take*, *to visit*.
2. Nas frases seguintes, substitua o infinito por um particípio e traduza de modo a que o sentido fique claro:
   Karl saw the actors enter the studio.
   He heard Mr. Hill explain the studio equipament.
   Karl watched the actors prepare a television play.
3. Encurte as seguintes frases, usando um particípio:
   As Karl wants to improve his English, he reads English papers.
   When Karl passed a newsagent's in Oxford Street, he bought The Times.
   As The Times is one of the best newspapers, Karl buys a copy every day.
   He sat down in the underground and opened the paper.
   When he had found the City News, he began to read.
   Though he did not understand every word, he liked to read the newspaper.
   The newspaper was very interesting, so Karl did not notice that the train was approaching Wood Green.
   When the train had reached the station, Karl had to get out.

Shopping in Town

Texto **22 A**

When Karl came to London he brought with him a long list of things we wanted to buy. Living with the Browns for some weeks now he had naturally got to know several of the local shops in the suburb: the tobacconist's, the chemist's, the stationer's, the confectioner's and (when he bought some flowers for Mrs. Brown) the florist's. But the things he needed now he wanted to buy in town. So he asked John to take him to the right shops. When he first showed John his long list, John burst out laughing.
«I hope you'll be able to get all these things through the customs, back home», he said.
«Come on, stop joking, and tell me where to go.»
«Can't I do that while we're going up to London?»
«All right then, let's start.»
«Do you want to go to Carnaby Street or the King's Road?» John asked, as they got into the underground. «Not for these things, I think. First I want a good English raincoat. I should like to get a Burberry. Isn't Burberry's shop in Haymarket?»
«Yes, we'll start from there. And what's the next item on you list?»
«A suit. I should like to have one made to order, even if it is more expensive. Where do you think I should go?»
«There are some very good men's tailors in Regent Street. That's not far from the Haymarket, so we'll go there afterwards.»
«Those are all the clothes I want to buy, but now come all these books and records.»
«For those I suggest going to Charing Cross Road. There you'll be able to find any book you want, old or new. And there are several record shops there too. Or we can go to the big one in Oxford Street, near Selfridge's.»
On entering Burberry's they see an assistant, who comes up to them and says: «What can I do for you, gentlemen?»
«I want a raincoat.»
«This way, please.»
Karl and John follow him to the rear of the large shop.
«What size do you take, sir?»
«I'm sorry, I don't know.»

«It doesn't matter, I can measure you: I'm sure we shall find one to fit you. Have you any special colour in mind?»

«Something not too light. I want a dark one.»

From the large stock of raincoats the assistant selects several for Karl to try on. Eventually he finds one that is exactly the right shade and fits well round the shoulders. The sleeves, are the right lenght, the coat, however, is a little too long.

«We can shorten it for you», the assistant suggests. «It will only take two days.»

After the tailor has taken his measurements and marked the raincoat accordingly Karl pays his bill. Highly satisfied he leaves the shop with John and together they head for Regent Street.

Notas gramaticais 22 B

1. O Gerúndio

> They stopped in front of the **building**.
> ITV is financed by **advertising**.
> There were many studios for **preparing** TV programmes.

Nestas frases, as formas em *-ing* não são evidentemente particípios. O artigo na primeira frase (*the*) e a preposição na segunda (*by*) indicam que se trata de formas substantivadas em *-ing*. Na terceira frase a preposição (*for*) indica a função de substantivo, ao passo que o complemento directo seguinte (*TV programmes*) faz a forma *-ing* parecer um verbo. Uma forma em *-ing* que tenha simultaneamente função substantiva e verbal, chama-se gerúndio. Para a grafia seguem-se as mesmas regras aplicadas ao particípio (vd. 13B1).

2. O Gerúndio como Sujeito e parte do Predicado

> **Seeing** is **believing**.
> It is worth while **visiting** the National Gallery.

Na primeira frase o gerúndio funciona como sujeito (*seeing*) e como parte do predicado (*believing*). Nos dois casos podia empregar-se o infinito com *to* (vd. 19B2).

Na segunda frase é o sujeito real (lógico). Como tal o gerúndio aparece sempre depois das expressões:

There is no	não se pode
it is (not) worth while ['wəːθ 'wail]	(não) vale a pena
it is no good	não serve de nada
it is no use	não serve de nada

3. O Gerúndio como Complemento Directo

> Stop **joking**.
> Karl had finished **reading**.

Depois dos seguintes verbos emprega-se sempre o gerúndio e não o infinito:

to avoid [əˈvɔid]	evitar
I cannot help	não posso deixar de

to delay [di'lei]	adiar
to have done with	acabar, resolver
to finish ['finiʃ]	terminar
to go on	continuar
to keep	continuar (a fazer alguma coisa)
to give up	desistir
to leave off	desistir
I do not mind	não me importo
to put off	adiar
to stop	acabar com
e outros	

4. O Gerúndio como complemento regido de preposição

> Jane is good at **writing** letters.
> She thanked Karl for **taking** her out to dinner.

O gerúndio é complemento depois de todos os verbos, adjectivos e substantivos ligados a preposição. São entre outros:

to complain of [kəm'plein]	queixar-se de
to depend on [di'pend]	confiar em
to delight in [di'lait]	ter prazer em
to despair of [dis'pɛə]	desesperar de
to look forward to ['fɔːwəd]	esperar com prazer
to object to [əb'dʒekt]	opor-se a
to prevent from [pri'vent]	impedir de
to rely on [ri'lai]	confiar em
to succeed in [sək'siːd]	ter êxito em
to thank for [θæŋk]	agradecer
to trouble about ['trʌbl]	preocupar-se com
to be accustomed to [ə'kʌstəmd]	estar habituado a
to be disappointed at [disə'pɔintid]	ficar desapontado com
to be fond of [fɔnd]	gostar muito de
to be good at	ser bom a (em)
to be keen on [kiːn]	gostar muito de; desejar
to be proud of [praud]	ter orgulho em
to be sick of [sik]	estar farto (*de uma coisa*)
to be in danger of ['deindʒə]	estar em perigo de
to be in the habit of ['hæbit]	estar habituado a
to be on the point of [pɔint]	estar prestes a

5. Gerúndio e Infinito

> They continued **talking**.
> **to talk**.
> He intended **going on**.
> **to go on**.

Com os seguintes verbos podemos usar o gerúndio ou o infinito:

to attempt [ə'tempt]	tentar
to begin	começar
to cease [siːs]	acabar de (com)
to continue [kən'tinjuː]	continuar (*a fazer alguma coisa*)
to hate [heit]	detestar
to intend [in'tend]	tencionar
to like [laik]	gostar de
to love [lʌv]	amar
to prefer [pri'fəː]	preferir
to regret [ri'gret]	lamentar
to remember [ri'membə]	lembrar-se de

6. O Pronome Relativo «that»
(vd. 4B5)

a)
> This is the paper **which** I like to read.
> This is the paper **that** I like to read.
> This is the paper I like to read.

Em orações relativas necessárias à compreensão da frase (*defining clauses*) é preferível *that* em vez de *who* e *which*. Este *that* quase sempre se omite quando é complemento directo da oração relativa. Estas orações relativas não são separadas por vírgula.

b)
> The Times is the **best** paper **(that)** you can buy.
> Tell me **everything (that)** you know about London.
> **It is** the Tower **that** Karl wants to visit.
> Karl wrote about the people and the places **(that)** he had seen.

That emprega-se ainda como pronome relativo:
1. depois de superlativos e expressões semelhantes como *the first*, *the last*, *the only*;
2. depois de pronomes indefinidos e numerais, como *all*, *something*, *anything*, *much*, *little*, *the same*, *nothing*;
3. numa ênfase determinada por *it is...*, *it was...*;
4. quando o pronome relativo se refere simultaneamente a pessoas e coisas.
Nos casos referidos em 1., 2. e 4. podemos omitir *that* se for complemento directo.

7. Lugar da preposição na oração relativa

> It is the Tower **in which** Karl is interested.
> It is the Tower **which** Karl is interested **in**.
> It is the Tower **that** Karl is interested **in**.
> It is the Tower Karl is interested **in**.

O verbo e a preposição formam uma unidade tal que dificilmente se separam. Daí resulta a colocação da preposição no fim da oração relativa. Com *that* só é possível esta construção. (Vd. lugar da preposição na passiva, 18B1 e 2.)

8. Preposições

> The typewriter is standing **on** the table.
> The book Is **on** the shelf.
> Karl is in London **on** a holiday.
> Here is a book **on** Shakespeare.

on

on l.: sobre, em
t.: a, em
c.: sobre

on foot	a pé
on the radio	no rádio
on T.V.	na televisão
on duty ['dju:ti]	de serviço
on his arrival [ə'raivəl]	à sua chegada

9. Verbos fortes e fracos irregulares

to draw	[ɔː]	drew	[uː]	drawn	[ɔː]	puxar; desenhar
to rise	[ai]	rose	[əu]	risen	[i]	levantar-se
to win	[i]	won	[ʌ]	won	[ʌ]	ganhar
to understand	[æ]	understood	[u]	understood	[u]	compreender

Exercícios **22 C**

1. Construa frases com as expressões e verbos dos n.ºˢ 2, 3 e 4 e 5 das NOTAS GRAMATICAIS.
2. Construa orações relativas com e sem *that* de acordo com os exemplos dos n.ºˢ 6 e 7 das NOTAS GRAMATICAIS.
3. Insira pronomes relativos adequados nas seguintes frases (omita-os quando possível):
   The paper __ Mr. Brown buys at the newsagent's is The Times.
   Jim, __ is John's friend, works at an office.
   Karl brought with him a list of things __ he wanted to buy.
   The things __ he needed now he wanted to buy in town.
   He finds a raincoat __ is exactly the right shade.
   The man __ comes up to them is the assistant.
   The coat, __ is a little too long, will be shortened.
   Karl is quite satisfied with all the things __ he has bought.

In the East End

Texto **23 A**

It was Sunday morning when John suggested to Karl they should visit Petticoat Lane and the East End of London. «They say, Karl, the East of London is where the money is made and the West is where it is spent. This doesn't mean, however, that you can't spend your money in the East. You certainly can, and I shall prove it by taking you to Petticoat Lane.»
«What a peculiar name, John. What sort of place is ti?»
«Wait until we're there and you'll see.»

They took the underground to Liverpool Street Station. And as John hadn't been to Petticoat Lane for some time he had to ask a policeman to direct them there.

«You needn't worry», the policeman answered, «just follow the crowd.»

After having been pushed along in a dense crowd of people into Middlesex Street, Karl realised what Petticoat Lane was, namely a street market. The narrow street was packed with stalls and stands. In front of the stalls dealers were shouting and calling out their wares, ofering for sale everything imaginable.

There was an endless variety extending from clothes to articles of toilet and jewellery, and from travel goods to household pets, together with all kinds of secondhand junk. It is well worth going to Petticoat Lane if only to listen to the eloquence of the dealers, whose hands, arms, mouth and face are constantly in motion to attract customers. Karl and John enjoyed it greatly.

«Where shall we go now, John?»

«I think we might walk down to the river.»

They walked through a district which had once been a depressing slum, with dirty streets and hold houses, but was now largely rebuilt with new flats. Eventually they reached the river and soon the most famous landmark of London lay before them, Tower Bridge, from where they could see up and down the Thames, and could also look at the great edifice of the Tower,

once both fortress and prison but now little more than a museum. «From here the Port of London extends eastwards for miles», John said. «Do you see the cranes and warehouses everywhere along the bank? And further down the river are all the big dicks, some of them as far away as Tilbury.»
Karl said he had expected to se more activity on the river.
«You forget it's Sunday. You should come here again on a workday. Then it's a hive of industry. But we must go and have lunch now. Then we could take a boat trip to Greenwich if you like, and visit the Observatory.»

Notas gramaticais 23 B

1. O Gerúndio com Sujeito próprio

> Do you mind **my smoking**?
> I do not mind **John's smoking**.
> I don't mind **John (him) smoking**.

Nestas frases o gerúndio tem sujeito próprio: «*Tu* importas-te que *eu* fume?» Este sujeito do gerúndio é expresso:
1. por um determinante possessivo,
2. pelo caso possessivo (na linguagem escrita) com nomes de pessoas,
3. pelo complemento directo (substantivo ou pronome pessoal).

2. O Gerúndio em vez de uma oração subordinada

> **On entering the shop** they see an assistant.
> They left the shop **without buying anything**.
> **Insted of going to Selfridge's** John and Karl went home.

O gerúndio ligado a uma preposição pode substituir uma oração subordinada (vd. o emprego do particípio, 21B4 e 5).
Essas preposições são:
    after   depois de
    on   a

in	durante
by	por meio de
without	sem
instead of [in'sted]	em vez de
in spite of [spait]	apesar de
through	por meio de

3. O emprego do Artigo Definido
(vd. 1B1)

a)
> **Eggs** are more expensive now than last month.
> **The eggs** we had for breakfast were very good.
> I prefer **tea** to **coffee**.
> **The tea** in my cup is already cold.
> **Life** is hard.
> Here is a bok about **the life** of Shakespeare.

O artigo definido individualiza um elemento de um conjunto de outros iguais. Por isso não se emprega com nomes no plural (*eggs*), com o nome de matéria (*tea, coffee*) e com abstractos (*life*). No entanto, se houver uma limitação de elementos, de matéria ou de noções abstractas no seu conjunto, é necessário empregar o artigo.

b)
> In **summer** we go to England.
> **The summer** of last year was very hot.
> **England** is an island.
> **The England** of Queen Victoria was a very rich country.

Não se emprega o artigo definido:
– com os dias da semana, meses, estações do ano, festas e refeições.
– com nomes de pessoas (*John Brown*), países (*Portugal*) (mas: *the United States*, *the Netherlands* ['neðələndz]), cidades (*London*), ruas (*Oxford Street*) (mas: *the High Street*), praças (*Trafalgar Square*), edifícios (*Westminster Abbey*), bem como designações de membros da família (*Father*) e conceitos religiosos (*God* [gɔd] Deus).

No entanto, se houver uma limitação, emprega-se o artigo.
The *Thames*, **the** *North Sea* (['nɔːθ siː] o mar do Norte), **the** *Alps* ([ælps] os Alpes).
Os nomes de rios, mares e montanhas são acompanhados de artigo definido.

c) | **Queen Victoria** was Queen of England.
    The Emperor Napoleon ruled over France.

Títulos seguidos de nome próprio não têm artigo; a não ser quando esses títulos não forem ingleses, como *emperor* (['empərə] imperador), *czar* ([zaː] czar).

d) | Tom is **at school**. (... na lição)
    The school is on the other side of the road.
    (O edifício da escola)

Os substantivos como *school*, *hospital* ['hɔspitl], *church* ([tʃəːtʃ] igreja), *prison* (['prizn] prisão), *bed*, *town*, etc. tomam artigo no seu significado concreto, mas não quando abstracto.

4. Preposições

> The train stopped **at** Bank Station.
> At six o'clock John arrived **at** Wood Green.
> John and Karl laughed **at** the film.

at

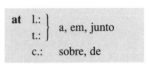

at school	na escola
at work	no trabalho
at Christmas ['krisməs]	no Natal
good at English	bom em inglês
not at all!	de nada!

> Mother sat **by** the table.
> Jane will be back **by** four o'clock.
> The quickest way to the City is **by** underground.

by

by	l.: junto de
	t.: até, perto de
	c.: de, por (passiva)

by land [lænd]	por terra
by day	de dia
day by day	dia a dia
by now	entretanto
by letter	por carta
by the way	a propósito

> Jane's office is **near** the Bank of England.
> The building is **near** completion. ([kəm'pliːʃən] pronto)

near

near l.: perto de

5. Verbos fortes e fracos irregulares

to drink [i]	**drank** [æ]	**drunk** [ʌ]	beber
to run [ʌ]	**ran** [æ]	**run** [ʌ]	correr
to write [ai]	**wrote** [əu]	**written** [i]	escrever
to lead [iː]	**led** [e]	**led** [e]	conduzir, levar
to sleep [iː]	**slept** [e]	**slept** [e]	dormir

Exercícios   23 C

1. Construa frases em que o gerúndio tenha sujeito próprio, de acordo com os exemplos do n.º 1 das NOTAS GRAMATICAIS. Utilize verbos de 22B2, 3 e 5.

2. Reduza as seguintes frases, empregando o gerúndio:
   When Karl left the station he bought a paper. When they reached Tower Bridge they had a look at the Tower. The Times is read by many people because it has good leading articles. After he left the station he had some money changed. Although he was in London for the first time he found his way. In the evening John and Karl wanted to return to Wood Green because they had been away for hours. Though they had left home early they were late for the film.

3. Empregue o artigo definido quando necessário:
   English people are fond of __ sport. John prefers __ cricket to all __ other games. Cricket is __ national game of the English. In __ spring John likes to play football. In __ summer of 1974 John was in Germany. __ school is near the station. On workdays the children are at __ school. __ England of today differs greatly from __ England of __ Queen Victoria.

By Boat to Greenwich

Texto **24 A**

«How right you are, John.»
«What do you mean, Karl?»
«You said it's relaxing to make a boat trip.»
«Yes, I didn't feel like walking any further at the moment.»
The two friends had gone on the riverboat after lunch. The morning had been rather tiring but sitting on the top deck in the breeze was refreshing and they could see the ships on the river and in the entrances to the docks. The boat was crowded, and a guide was giving a commentary over a loud-speaker.
«This is where the Pilgrim Fathers set sail from for America in 1620», he told them as they passed the Mayflower Inn in Rotherhithe. And later «That is the site of the old Deptford naval dockyard, where Sir Francis Drake was knighted by Queen Elizabeth the First, and the Russian Emperor, Peter the Great, came to study shipbuilding in 1698.»

At last they reached Greenwich. «The building in front of you is the Royal Naval College», the guide said, «and above it on the hill is the famous observatory from which comes the expression «Greenwich Time». The next boat back to the Tower will leave in an hour's time.»

«That just gives us time to walk up to the Observatory and see the line of the Greenwich Meridian», said John. They climbed up the hill and at the top he was able to take a photograph of Karl standing with one foot in the eastern and the other in the western hemisphere! But unfortunately there was no time to go inside the historic Observatory and see the old telescopes.

As they got off the boat back at the Tower Karl heard loud voices in the distance. «It's the speakers on Tower Hill», John told him. «This is one of the places like Hyde Park where people are free to come and speak on any subject under the sun.» They joined the crowd, and Karl stood fascinated by the wildness of some of the speeches and the good-humoured tolerance of the audience, until at last John exclaimed «I'm thirsty. How about a drink?» So off they went to a nearby pub.

Notas gramaticais 24 B

1. O Conjuntivo

> John **visits** Germany.

Esta frase expressa um facto, uma realidade. O verbo está no Indicativo (forma da realidade).

> **Go** and **visit** the Browns.

Esta frase expressa uma exortação, uma ordem. Os verbos estão no Imperativo (vd. 6B1).

> If I **were** you, I should visit England.

A oração subordinada começada por *if* expressa uma possibilidade imaginada, não realizada. O verbo está no Conjuntivo (forma de hipótese, de possibilidade).
As três frases são exemplos de três expressões diferentes: realidade – exortação – possibilidade.
Em inglês há apenas com formas especiais do conjuntivo, como por ex. na frase com *if, I/he/she/it were* – eu/ele/ela fosse, estivesse.
As restantes formas são substituídas pelas correspondentes do indicativo. Além disso, empregam-se perífrases com verbos auxiliares irregulares (vd. 25B).

2. O discurso directo e indirecto

Há duas possibilidades de transmitir as palavras de alguém:
a) O Karl disse: «Agrada-me estar em Londres.»
O discurso directo repete a frase à letra.
b) O Karl disse, que lhe agradava estar em Londres.
O discurso indirecto transmite as palavras do emissor com as daquele que as pronuncia, usando o indicativo:

Discurso Directo	Discurso Indirecto
Karl **says**: «I **am** glad to be here.»	Karl **says** that he **is** glad to be here.
Karl **said**: «I **am** glad to be here.»	Karl **said** that he **was** glad to be here.
Karl **said**: «I **had** a nice trip.»	Karl **said** that he **had had** a nice trip.

Se a **frase introdutória** tiver o verbo no **presente** (*Karl says*), **no discurso indirecto** o verbo aparece **no tempo** usado **no discurso directo**.
Se a **frase introdutória** estiver no **pretérito** aparece também o **pretérito no discurso indirecto.**
As formas do pretérito são:
Past Tense – Past Perfect – Future-in-the-past (vd. 9B1, 6, 7, 10B1, 3, 11B3, 5, 6, 12B4).

3. Emprego do Artigo indefinido
(vd. 1B1)

a)
> Jane is **a** secretary.
> Elizabeth is Queen of England.
> John had tea, toast and butter for breakfast.

O artigo indefinido é uma forma menos forte do numeral *one*. Serve para designar uma de pessoas ou coisas pertencentes a um grupo de elementos semelhantes. Por isso não se emprega com substantivos que referem algo que só existe uma vez, ou com nomes de substâncias.

b)
> He works five days **a week**.
> It is thirty pence **a pound**.

Com referência a medidas e tempo o artigo indefinido designa a unidade («... por semana», «... por libra»).

4. Preposições

> Two years **ago**, I saw London for the first time.
> Karl has been in London **since** the beginning of the month.

ago t.: há (a contar do presente)   **since** t.: há, desde (a partir de um ponto do passado)

ago coloca-se sempre depois do período de tempo referido; liga-se ao Past Tense.
since liga-se ao Present Perfect. (Vd. 11B3, 4.)

5. Verbos fortes e fracos irregulares

to see	[iː]	saw	[ɔː]	seen	[iː]	ver
to bring	[i]	brought	[ɔː]	brought	[ɔː]	trazer
to learn	[əː]	learnt*	[əː]	learnt*	[əː]	aprender
to smell	[e]	smelt*	[e]	smelt*	[e]	cheirar

* Existem igualmente formas regulares.

Exercícios **24 C**

1. Passe o discurso directo para o indirecto:
   John asks: «Where is the letter from Karl?»
   Mother answers: «There's his letter on the table.»
   John said: «I hope you had a good flight.»
   Karl replied: «It was very quick.»
   Mr. Brown asked: «What is wrong?»
   Mrs. Brown answered: «I saw a terrible accident.»
   Jane wanted to know: «Was anyone hurt?»
   Mrs. Brown said: «An old man was hit by one of the wheels.»
   The guide explained: «This is the Woolsack.»
   Karl exclaimed: «How right you are, John.»
2. Insira o artigo indefinido quando necessário:
   John is __ mechanic and Jane is __ secretary. They work five days __ week. They had __ nice meal with __ roast beef and __ wine. Victoria was __ Queen of England. He is __ good friend of mine.
3. Forme frases com as seguintes expressões:
   once a week, twice a day, once a year, four times a month, sixty pence a pound.

Interesting Places around London

Texto **25 A**

Karl had already seen many of London's famous sights and now before going back to Germany he wanted to visit some of the places in the surroundings. So he was very glad when one evening John's uncle, who worked at the Information Centre of the British Tourist Authority, came to tell him about places to visit in the Home Counties, the counties within easy reach of London. To bring his words to life Uncle Brian illustrated his talk with coloured slides. «One place you must visit is the ancient borough of Windsor in Berkshire. Since the time of William the Conqueror, who ascended the English throne in 1066, the magnificent royal residence of Windsor Castle has overlooked the Thames Valley. The castle is open to the public when the Queen is not in residence. Every lover or connoisseur of architecture should see St. George's

Chapel, which is the burial-place of many of our monarchs, and one of the most perfect examples of the Perpendicular style. And it is worthwhile visiting the State Apartments, which contain a superb collection of pictures. After visiting the castle you may like to spend some time on the terraces or enjoying the view from the Round Tower.

Across the river, on the northern bank, is Eton College, the most famous public school in England. This school was founded by King Henry VI early in the fifteenth century and some of the buildings erected then have been preserved. A visit to the School Yard and the Chapel is very rewarding. Although the boys today no longer wear the traditional tophats, Eton jackets and tailcoats are still worn. Many of England's famous politicians and diplomats have been Old Etonians.» Uncle also spoke about some places in the Thames Valley which can be visited on the way to Windsor, such as the royal palace of Hampton Court. «Begun by Cardinal Wolsey in 1515 it was taken over by Henry VIII after the Cardinal's fall, and one of his six wives is said still to haunt it. Round the palace there are splendid gardens, with a very old vine and a maze. And from Hampton Court one can go on to the meadow of Runnymede by the Thames, where the Magna Carta was signed.»

Uncle's last pictures took Karl north of London to St. Alban's in Hertfordshire. The site of Verulamium, the most important Roman town in the south of England, is a short distance to the West of the present town. The walls of the Cathedral, which is one of the earliest Norman churches in the country, contain Roman tiles and bricks. And close to St. Alban's is Hatfield House, the stately home of the Cecil family and once the childhood home of Queen Elizabeth I.

Uncle would have liked to show slides of Oxford and Cambridge too, but there was no time. And as he said to Karl afterwards: «You must leave some places to see on your next visit to England.»

Notas gramaticais   25 B

O conjuntivo é empregado em orações subordinadas, mas é quase sempre substituído por verbos defectivos (*may*, *might*, *shall*, *should*) ou, na linguagem comum, pelo indicativo.

1. Orações concessivas

> **Though the observatory is interesting** they did not go in.
> **Wherever we may go**, we shall take a guide along.

As orações concessivas são introduzidas por:
(al)though embora   whatever o que quer que
however   por (muito)   whoever   quem quer que

Nestas orações emprega-se *may* no presente e *might* no passado ou no presente do indicativo. A oração subordinada tem geralmente o verbo no futuro ou no presente.

2. Orações condicionais

As orações condicionais são introduzidas por:
if   se   as long as   com a condição de
unless a não ser que   provided (that) [prə'vaidid]   desde que

a)
> John will come **if you ask him**.
> O John vem se lhe pedires.

Algo se passa se a condição se realizar.
A oração subordinada tem o verbo no futuro e a de *if* no presente.

b)
> John would come **if you asked him**.
> O John vinha se lhes pedisses.

Aqui o resultado é improvável, porque a realização da condição é incerta.
A oração subordinada tem o verbo no condicional e a de *if* no pretérito.

c)
> John would have come **if you had asked him**.
> O John tinha vindo se lhe tivesses pedido.

Aqui foi excluída a realização da condição, pelo que o resultado está fora de questão.
A oração subordinada tem o verbo no condicional composto e a de *if* no pretérito mais que perfeito.

3. Expressões de desejo

> *a)* God **save** the Queen. ([seiv] salvar, guardar)
> *b)* I wish **it were true**. Linguagem comum:... **it was true**.
> *c)* John wished **that his friend might come back next year**.

a) Em frases já fixas pela tradição o conjuntivo expressa um desejo.
b) Desejos não realizados são expressos no pretérito ou no mais que perfeito.
c) Desejos realizáveis são expressos com *may* (quando o verbo da oração subordinante estiver no presente) e *might* (quando aquele verbo estiver no pretérito).

4. Orações finais

> John **takes / took** an expensive ticket, **so that he may / might see better**.
> John took an expensive ticket **(in order) to see better**.

As orações finais são introduzidas por:
(so) that   para que   in order that   para que
O verbo da oração final é *may* (se o da oração subordinante estiver no presente) ou *might* (se aquele verbo estiver no pretérito).
Muitas vezes a oração final é substituída por uma infinitiva.

5. Preposições

> They were **inside** the building.
> The school is **outside** the town.

× inside   × outside

inside l.: dentro de
outside l.: fora de

6. Verbos fortes e fracos irregulares

to eat	[iː]	**ate**	[e]	**eaten**	[iː]	comer	
to shake	[ei]	**shook**	[u]	**shaken**	[ei]	abanar, sacudir	
to spend	[e]	**spent**	[e]	**spent**	[e]	gastar; passar (tempo)	

Exercícios **25 C**

1. Construa orações concessivas com as conjunções apresentadas em B1 das NOTAS GRAMATICAIS.
2. Construa duas orações condicionais de acordo com cada um dos três exemplos apresentados em B2 das NOTAS GRAMATICAIS.
3. Construa cinco expressões de desejo de acordo com os exemplos apresentados em B3 das NOTAS GRAMATICAIS.
4. Construa dez orações finais de acordo com os exemplos apresentados em B4 das NOTAS GRAMATICAIS.

London Theatres

Texto **26 A**

Thinking of his plan to take Jane to the theatre Karl looks at the section on theatres in a London entertainments guide. This is what he reads:

«Few cities in the world can compare with London as a centre for drama and music. In the field of drama the genius of Shakespeare has prevailed all these centuries. Although the last five decades have produced many excellent playwrights, the human insight and the great dramatic skill of that actor-poet have remained unsurpassed. And we owe it to his genius that, when he retired from London to spend the evening of his life in the countryside where he was born, he left behind a city which had developed through him a thirst for the drama. What wonder then that today we find as many as fifty theatres of every kind and quality in central London. Although it has undergone much reconstruction, the most recent having been carried out in the early nineteenth century, the Theatre Royal in Drury Lane is the oldest of London's present-day theatres. It was opened in 1663 and still stands on its original site. It is one of the largest theatres in the world. Nowadays large-scale musical productions are performed on its vast stage. It would, in fact, create a sensation if an impresario were to break with tradition and have a 'straight' play performed on its stage.

Straight plays are the tradition at another theatre with a long history, the Haymarket Theatre. But other theatres that share Drury Lane's reputation for elaborate musicals are Her Majesty's and The Palace Theatre.

So many of London's theatres are situated in the district round Shaftesbury Avenue that this is sometimes called 'Theatreland'. But one very famous one is not. The National Theatre is now housed in its new building by the South bank of the river and produces there every year a first-class repertory of important modern plays as well as Shakespearean and classical drama.

London's theatres have something to offer to every taste. Covent Garden, for instance, attracts the admirer of grand opera, and of ballet, which can also be seen at the Coliseum and Sadler's Wells. Theatres like the Palladium and Victoria Palace specialise in variety and revue. And there are all kinds of smaller theatres concentrating on modern or 'experimental' productions. Above all, these facilities can be enjoyed at any time of the year. There is no 'dead' season in London.»

Notas gramaticais **26 B**

1. A forma progressiva e o tempo simples

> Karl **was writing** a letter home, when his friend **came** in.
> What **have** you **been doing** today?

A forma progressiva expressa uma acção que está a decorrer. («O Karl estava a escrever uma carta, quando...» «Que andaste a fazer hoje?»)

> Yesterday Karl **wrote** a letter home.
> What **have** you **done** today?

Pelo contrário, um tempo simples expressa que o interese do locutor só incide sobre o próprio facto e não sobre o decurso do processo. (Ontem o Karl escreveu uma carta...» «Que fizeste hoje?»)

2. Salientar o verbo

> *a)* Karl **was saying** that he found London fascinating.
> *b)* Karl **did enjoy** his trip ([trip] passeio) on the river.
> *c)* Let's **have a drink**.

Para salientar o verbo existem as seguintes possibilidades:
a) a forma progressiva em vez do tempo simples («O Karl frisou que...»),
b) emprego do verbo *to do* como enfático («O passeio pelo rio agradou *de facto* ao Karl.»),
c) *to have* ligado a um substantivo em vez do verbo simples:
to have a drink (em vez de *to drink*)
to have a smoke (em vez de *to smoke*)

3. Preposições

> **During** their meal he talked about what he had seen.
> From here you can see **for** miles around.
> John worked **for** six hours.
> He looked **for** a taxi.

during t.: durante

for l.: por, ao longo de, para
t.: durante
c.: por, por causa de, a, com

for breakfast — ao pequeno-almoço
to go for a walk — ir passear
to start for London — partir para Londres
for this reason ['riːzn] — por esta razão
for fear (of) — com medo (de)

4. Verbos fortes e fracos irregulares

to fall	[ɔː]	**fell**	[e]	**fallen**	[ɔː]	cair
to shine	[ai]	**shone**	[ɔ]	**shone**	[ɔ]	brilhar
to burn	[əː]	**burnt***	[əː]	**burnt***	[əː]	queimar
to let	[e]	**let**	[e]	**let**	[e]	deixar, permitir
to spoil	[ɔi]	**spoilt***	[ɔi]	**spoilt***	[ɔi]	estragar

* também existem formas regulares

Exercícios 26 C

1. Construa frases na forma progressiva e com tempo simples, de acordo com os exemplos apresentados em B1 das NOTAS GRAMATICAIS.
2. Construa frases de acordo com os exemplos apresentados em B2a–c das NOTAS GRAMATICAIS.

Goodbye to Karl

Texto **27 A**

It was Karl's last day in England. He had had a pleasant evening with Jane at the theatre the day before, and now he was having a farewell meal with the whole family at home. He had grown very fond of them all.
«We shall be sorry to lose you», said Mr. Brown. «We've enjoyed having you with us and hope you'll come back and stay with us again.»
«I'd like to very much», replied Karl. «You've all been extremely kind to me, and thanks to you I've been very happy here and able to learn a lot more English. You've helped me to understand English people, too, and enjoy their sense of humour.»
«Talking of sense of humour», said John, «there's an old joke I want to tell you, to see whether your English is good enough to understand it, and make you laugh. Here it is.»
«An Englishman once crossed into Red Indian territory and saw a very old Indian sitting on a stone, deep in thought and smoking a pipe of peace. The Englishman walked up to him and lifting his arm, greeted the Indian according to tradition by saying, 'How!' – The Indian answered 'How!' – 'What are you doing here?' the Englishman asked. – 'I'm thinking'. – 'What are you thinking about?' – 'The details of my long life. I can remember everything, though I'm 99 now. You can ask me anything, I shall prove that I'm right'. – 'All right', thought the Englishman, 'I might as well', and he asked: 'What did you have for breakfast on 20th July, 1900?' – 'Eggs', was the Indian's prompt reply. The Englishman was so baffled that he went away, not saying another word. Two years later he came back to the same territory, and there was the Indian again, sitting on the same stone and smoking a pipe of peace. So the Englishman walked up to him again and said 'How!', whereupon the Indian answered 'Fried'.»
The others all laughed but it was some time before Karl could see the joke and understand the double meaning of «How» in the story.

«Yes», he said, «obviously I still have a great deal to learn, but that only makes me all the more determined to come back again, if you'll let me.»

«Let's drink to your next visit then», said Mr. Brown. And they all raised their glasses.

Notas gramaticais 27 B

1. Passagem de um estado para outro

> Jane **became** angry because she had to wait.
> John **became** a mechanic.
> What **has become** of him?
> His hair **has turned** white.
> It **grew** darker and darker.
> You will understand when you **grow** older.
> Karl **had grown** fond of the family.
> If you **get** tired you can go to bed.

Em inglês a passagem de um estado para outro é expressa pelos verbos *to become*, *to turn*, *to grow* ou *to get*. Além disso existem ainda numerosas expressões idiomáticas, como por ex.:

to fall ill	adoecer
to fall due	vencer (o pagamento)
to go bad	deteriorar-se
to come true	bater certo

2. «Deixar», «Mandar», «Fazer com que»

a)
> **Let** me help you
> He **allowed** / **permitted** John take the book.

Com o sentido de «permitir» diz-se:
to let seguido de infinito sem *to* (vd. 20B2),
to allow, *to permit* seguidos de infinito com *to* (vd. 20B3).

b)
> John's joke **made** the others laugh.
> The Indian **caused** the Englishman to return.
> Mr. Morrow **had** Jane write to New York.
> Karl **got** John to explain the joke.

«Mandar», «fazer com que» diz-se:
to make e – em frases afirmativas – *to have* seguidos de infinito sem *to* (vd. 20B2),
to cause [kɔːz], *to command*, *to get*, *to order* seguidos de infinito com *to* (vd. 20B3).

> He **ordered the waiter to serve** the drinks.
> He **ordered the drinks to be served**.

Em sentido passivo o infinito toma a forma passiva (vd. 19B4).

c)
> He **had** a new suit **made**. (Ele mandou fazer...)
> She **got** her hair **cut**. (Ela mandou cortar...)

«Mandar fazer» pode ser expresso por **to have** ou **to get** seguidos de particípio passado.

d) Há um conjunto de verbos que podem ter um significado duplo:

to fly	voar		fazer voar
to enter	entrar		incorporar (numa lista)
to run	correr	ou	fazer andar
to sink	afundar-se		afundar
to grow	crescer		fazer crescer, cultivar

A partir de alguns **adjectivos**, acrescentando **-en,** formam-se verbos com o significado de «passar a um estado»:

hard	— **to harden**	endurecer
strong	— **to strengthen**	fortalecer
weak	— **to weaken**	enfraquecer
soft	— **to soften**	atenuar, mitigar

mas:

warm	— **to warm**	aquecer

3. Ordem das palavras

> S. P. C. D.
> We have breakfast.
> Do we have breakfast?
> If we have breakfast...

A ordem das palavras obedece a um sistema fixo. A ordem normal na afirmativa, na interrogativa, na subordinante e na subordinada é:

> Sujeito — Predicado — Complemento Directo

O predicado e o complemento directo não podem ser separados por complementos (vd. 11B7).

> I gave him my book.
> I gave my book to him.

Mas se a frase tiver um complemento indirecto, este precede o directo, a não ser que, por uma questão de ênfase, seja acompanhado de *to* (vd. 2B3 e 5, 17B4).
Os desvios desta ordem estabelecida são muito raros. A inversão do sujeito (predicado – sujeito) verifica-se:

a)
> Along **dashed the car**.
> There **comes John**.
> Wonderful **was the sight**.
> John went home and so **did I**.

– para ênfase de partes da frase;

b)
> Seldom **did I** see such an interesting building.
> John had not seen the accident, nor **had Karl**.

– depois de expressões negativas e restritivas no início da frase. Essas expressões podem ser:

seldom ['sɛldəm]	raramente	no sooner...than	
rarely ['rɛəli]	raramente	scarcely...when ['skɛəsli]	mal
never ['nevə]	nunca	hardly...when	
in vain [vein]	em vão		
little ['litl]	pouco	not only...but (also)	não só... mas também
nor [nɔː]	nem		

c) **Were John** here, he would show me the way.
Had he seen the accident, he would have helped.

– em orações condicionais sem *if*, com *had* e *were* (vd. 25B2);

d) Long **live the Queen!**

– em expressões de desejo formais (vd. 25B3).

4. Preposições

They went north **of** the river.
The weather had been fine **of** late. (of late = ultimamente)
This bridge is made **of** wood.

> **of** l.: de
> t.: em, de
> c.: a, de, em

to be afraid of	ter medo de
to be proud of	estar orgulhoso de
to be ashamed of [ə'ʃeimd]	ter vergonha de
to die of [dai]	morrer de
to think of	pensar em
to smell of [smel]	cheirar a

He fell **off** his seat.
The ships met **off** Dover.
All day long John was **off** form. (= mal-disposto)

off

off l.: afastado de
c.: além de

5. Verbos fortes e fracos irregulares

to fight	[ai]	fought	[ɔː]	fought	[ɔː]	lutar
to sing	[i]	sang	[æ]	sung	[ʌ]	cantar
to burst	[əː]	burst	[əː]	burst	[əː]	estalar, rebentar
to light	[ai]	lit*	[i]	lit*	[i]	acender
to spread	[e]	spread	[e]	spread	[e]	espalhar(-se)

* Também existem formas regulares

Exercícios   **27 C**

1. Construa frases com os verbos apresentados nos n.º 1 e 2 das NOTAS GRAMATICAIS.
2. Use a inversão do sujeito em orações condicionais sem *if*.
3. Construa frases começando com as expressões negativas e restritivas indicadas no n.º 3b.
4. Conte a anedota sobre o índio.

First Impressions of New York

Texto   **28 A**

Shortly after Karl had left London to return home to Germany there was another departure in the Brown family. Some time before, Jane had been invited to spend several weeks in America working in her firm's New York office, so she too left England, almost beside herself with excitement. After flying across the Atlantic she at last caught sight of the distant outline of the great city. The skyscrapers of Manhattan, the chief island between the Hudson and the East River, reached high up into the sky. And on an island in the harbour the Statue of Liberty greeted newcomers, holding up her torch and looking out over the waters of the ocean.

After landing at Kennedy Airport Jane passed through the customs and hailed a taxi to take her to a hotel that had been recommended to her.
Next morning the phone rang in her hotel room. «There's a Mr. Beckett waiting for you in the lobby.»
«Thank you. I'll be down in a minute.»
When Jane reached the lobby a man rose from one of the seats. «Miss Brown? I'm Bill Beckett, Johnson and Howard's New York agent.»
Jane shook hands. «I'm very glad to see you, Mr. Beckett, and thank you so much for your kind offer to show me round New York.»
«Don't mention it, just let's get going.»

Sitting in a taxi and driving through the crowded streets, which were like rocky gorges between the towering buildings, Mr. Beckett told Jane something of the history of New York. «The city is now more than 300 years old. Its history began in 1609, when Henry Hudson, the famous explorer, tried to find the northwest passage to Asia and discovered this place. He sailed up the river that now bears his name. The first settlers here were Dutch colonists, who bought the island of Manhattan from the

Indians and called their settlement New Amsterdam. This was in 1620. Forty years later, however, the English captured the town and changed its name to New York.»

As the taxi stopped outside the Empire State Building Mr. Beckett interrupted his talk. Jane looked up at the high front of the building with its rows of innumerable windows. It seemed to vanish in the clouds. «Well», she said, «this *is* a skyscraper indeed.»

«It isn't our tallest skyscraper any more», said Mr. Beckett. «The World Trade Center is higher, and the Sears Tower in Chicago is higher still. But I still think this has the best view. It's 1250 feet high, without the TV tower, and has 102 stories. 18,000 people work in it but it can house about 25,000.»

There were many lifts in the building. They took one going up to the Observation Tower. «In America we call this an 'elevator', not a 'lift', as you do in England», Mr. Beckett explained. «And we don't say 'autumn', we say 'fall'. A 'pavement' is a 'sidewalk', a 'motor-car' an 'automobile' and a 'car park' a 'parking place'. You see, there's something almost amounting to an American language, which differs in many ways from the British.»

After they had reached the Observation Tower they looked out over the great mass of buildings and Jane stood montionless for quite a long time. «It's really fantastic», she said at last. «I've never seen anything like it.»

Notas sobre a língua inglesa
e notas gramaticais **28 B**

1. O Inglês americano

A evolução do inglês americano, que se distanciou do britânico, tem no fundo quatro razões principais: o afastamento geográfico da terra-mãe, o dialecto dos primeiros colonizadores, a imigração de indivíduos de línguas diversas e finalmente a separação política da Inglaterra como resultado da Guerra da Independência (1776).

Desde então, o americano tem vindo a tomar, cada vez mais marcadamente, uma forma linguística própria. Surgiram diferenças de pronúncia e grafia e foram introduzidas palavras de outras línguas, em espe-

cial do francês, espanhol e alemão, e ainda do chinês e das línguas dos índios. De início a influência linguística partia da Inglaterra. Hoje, pelo contrário – em consequência do desenvolvimento político e económico – o americano está a impor-se cada vez mais.
Neste livro, até aqui, foram apresentados exclusivamente a grafia, pronúncia e vocabulário britânicos. Nas últimas lições vão ser apresentadas algumas características do americano, para esclarecer as diferenças mais importantes entre os dois ramos da língua.

2. Diferenças de vocabulário

Britânico	Americano	Português
bank-note	bill	nota (de banco)
biscuit ['biskit]	cooky ['kuki]	biscoito
chemist	druggist ['drʌgist]	farmacêutico
cinema	movies ['muːviz]	cinema
fortnight ['fɔːtnait]	two weeks	quinze dias
goods train	freight train [freit]	comboio de mercadorias
ground floor	first floor	rés-do-chão
lift	elevator ['eliveitə]	elevador
lorry ['lɔri]	truck [trʌk]	camião
pavement	sidewalk	passeio (para peões)
petrol ['petrəl]	gas(oline) ['gæs(əliːn)]	gasolina
railway	railroad	caminho-de-ferro
sweets	candy ['kændi]	rebuçados
tin [tin]	can [kæn]	lata
torch	flashlight ['flæʃlait]	lâmpada de bolso
tram [træm]	streetcar	eléctrico

3. Termos de outras línguas

Os termos de origem índia vivem principalmente em nomes topográficos: Massachusetts, Utah, Mississippi, Iowa.
Termos provenientes do alemão:
beergarden, blitz(krieg), delicatessen, kindergarten, noodle, sauerkraut, schnitzel, volkswagen;

Do espanhol: ranch, mustang, sombrero, canyon, corral, tornado, sierra;
Do francês: prairie, depot, toboggan, pumpkin;
Do chinês: to flop (dormitar), to kowtow (fazer uma vénia profunda, rastejar).

4. Preposições

> They came **past** many high buildings.
> It is half **past** nine.
> This is **past** doubt. ([daut] dúvida)
> The ship sailed **along** the coast. ([kəust] costa)

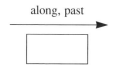

along, past

along	l.: ao longo de
past	l.: junto de
	t.: depois
	c.: para além de

5. Verbos fortes e fracos irregulares

to find	[ai]	found	[au]	found	[au]	encontrar
to sink	[i]	sank	[æ]	sunk	[ʌ]	afundar-se
to lose	[uː]	lost	[ɔ]	lost	[ɔ]	perder
to teach	[iː]	taught	[ɔː]	taught	[ɔː]	ensinar

Note:
	to find	found	found	encontrar
	to found	founded	founded	fundar

Exercícios **28 C**

Recapitulação da formação e do emprego dos tempos (Lições 9-12):
1. Nas frases seguintes empregue o Past Tense ou o Present Perfect dos verbos entre parêntesis:
   Some months ago, an American friend of the Browns __ Jane to visit New York. (to invite)
   Last week she __ London. (to leave)
   For some hours she __ across the ocean. (to fly)
   She just __ at the airport. (to arrive)

When Jane enters the hotel lobby, Mr. Beckett ___ for some minutes. (to wait)
The history of New York ___ in 1609. (to begin)
Henry Hudson ___ the island of Manhattan. (to discover)
The first settlers ___ Dutch colonists. (to be)
All through its history New York ___ an important place. (to be)
The English ___ the name of the Dutch settlement to New York. (to change)
Today Jane and Mr. Beckett ___ through the streets. (to drive)
Jane ___ in New York now for two days. (to be).

2. De cada duas frases contrua cinco de acordo com o exemplo seguinte (do texto):
   After Karl *had left* London, Jane *went* to America.
   Before Jane *went* to America, Karl *had left* London.
   Recapitulação da forma progressiva (Lição 13).

3. Insira nas seguintes frases os verbos entre parêntesis, empregando a forma progressiva quando necessário:
   Look, the plane ___ the airport. (to approach)
   When the plane ___ the coast ([kəust] costa), the skyline of New York ___ into view. (to reach, to come)
   The Statue of Liberty ___ on an island in the harbour. (to stand)
   While the passengers ___ the plane, many taxis ___ in front of the airport building. (to leave, to drive up)
   Hundreds of people ___ at the airport to await the newcomers. (to stand)
   Jane ___ in her hotel room, when suddenly the telephone ___. (to sit, to ring).
   When Jane ___ the hotel lobby, Mr. Beckett ___ in a chair. (to enter, to sit)
   Mr. Beckett ___ about the American language, when the lift suddenly ___. (to speak, to stop)
   When Jane ___ over the great mass of buildings, she did not speak for quite some time. (to look)

4. De cada uma das frases seguintes forme dez de acordo com os exemplos apresentados:
   Mr. Beckett was speaking of New York, when suddenly the taxi stopped at the Empire State Building.
   While Jane was looking at the view from the Observation Tower, thousands of vehicles were passing below her.

A Bird's-eye View of New York

Texto **29 A**

It was a wonderful day. The sky was blue. Only a few white clouds were moving slowly towards the west. The air being clear, Jane could see as far as fifty miles in every direction. Manhattan under her was a forest of skyscrapers, and round it on the other banks of the two rivers, Greater New York stretched far and wide.

«Within a radius of fifty miles», Mr. Beckett said, «about twelve and a half million people live. But now look down on Manhattan. The island is 13 miles long and about two miles wide, and has two million inhabitants, whereas Greater New York has a population of eight millions. There are 80 languages spoken here. Going through the different quarters of New York you'll learn to understand why America has been called 'the melting-pot of nations'. And talking of nations that's the United Nations building over there.»

«How systematically Manhattan has been built!» Jane exclaimed.

«Yes, it's a system of blocks, a regular pattern of squares. The roads running from north to south, from one end of the island to the other, are called 'avenues'. The roads running from west to east, from the Hudson to the East River, cross them at right angles. They are called 'streets'. Avenues and streets have no special names as a rule, they are simply numbered: First Avenue, Second Avenue, Twenty-First Street, Twenty-Second Street and so on. If you want to visit a friend in New York you needn't ask your way, you only have to count.»

«I know at least one street which has a special name – Broadway.»

«Yes, that runs from the northwest to the southeast, forming a kind of diagonal line which doesn't fit into the regular pattern. Look, there it is, down there. And around it, of course, are all the big places of entertainment, the theaters, cinemas and so on. Broadway is also an important shopping street. But you really ought to see it at night when it's brilliantly lit up. Then we call it 'The Great White Way'».

«Where is Wall Street?»

«Over there, towards the south. It's a rather small street but an important one. As you know the New York Stock Exchange is there, so it's the center of our commercial and financial life.»
«Why is it called Wall Street?»
«Well, I told you about the first settlers, the Dutch colonists. They had built a fence there, a wall, to protect their settlement against their enemies and against wild beasts. There were wolves and bears here in those days.»
Jane turned towards the north. She pointed to a large patch of green in the middle of the island. «What's that?»
«That's Central Park, west of Fifth Avenue and between 59th and 110th Streets. It's a very big park with lakes in it, and a zoo. And near the Park runs Park Avenue with all its elegant hotels and rich people's houses.»
«And what about the poorer parts? Where's the negro quarter, Harlem, for instance?»
«Oh, that's further north, beyond the Park and reaching up to the Harlem River. The name 'Harlem' by the way is taken from Haarlem in Holland and goes back to the time of the Dutch colonists. The eastern part of the district is sometimes called 'Spanish Harlem' because that's where most of the Puerto Ricans live. I expected you know already that Harlem isn't a safe place to wander about in alone.»

Notas sobre a língua inglesa
e notas gramaticais   29 B

1. Particularidades da pronúncia americana

A pronúncia do inglês americano é bastante uniforme, apesar da vasta extensão dos Estados Unidos. Embora também existam diferenças dialectais, não são tão vincadas como por exemplo na Inglaterra, Alemanha e outros países. Além disso, algumas particularidades regionais vão sendo cada vez mais esbatidas pelas circunstâncias da vida moderna (grande movimentação, influência da rádio, do cinema, da televisão, da imprensa, etc.).

Em comparação com o inglês britânico, verificam-se muitas diferenças de pronúncia.

2. A pronúncia das sílabas não acentuadas

Nas sílabas não acentuadas verificam-se diferenças bastante marcadas em relação ao inglês britânico:

	Britânico	**Americano**	
advertisement	[əd'vɜːtismənt]	['ædvɚ'taizmənt]	anúncio
dictionary	['dikʃənri]	['dikʃə'neri]	dicionário
interesting	['intristiŋ]	['intə'restiŋ]	
secretary	['sekrətri]	['sɛkrə'tɛri]	

3. Tendência para a nasalação

Uma característica especial do inglês americano é o *nasal twang* ['neizəl 'twæŋ], a tendência para nasalar as vogais e não apenas antes de *m*, *n* e *ng*.

4. Diferenças em casos isolados

a) No americano o *r* é pronunciado em casos em que é mudo no inglês britânico, como em *arm*, *finger* e *fur*. Mas este *r* americano é diferente do britânico; tem o ponto de articulação na parte posterior da cavidade bucal ([ɹ]).
A diferença é muito nítida em

clerk   [klɑːk]   britânico
                            [kləːɹk]   americano

b) Em numerosas palavras americanas o grupo [juː] é pronunciado simplesmente [uː]:
new, *duty*, *student*, *tune*, *nude*, *suit*.

c) Em americano, o [ɑː] britânico passa a [æ] antes de *f*, *s*, *n*, *th*:
after, *ask*, *path*, *laugh*, *pass*, *can't*.

d) Em americano, o [ɔ] britânico passa a [ɑ]:
box, *dog*, *God*, *lot*, *often*, *pot*, *sock*.

e) O grupo [ʌr] do inglês britânico é pronunciado [ər] em americano:
courage, *hurry*, *worry*.

5. Preposições

> Jane stood **beside** Mr. Beckett.
> She was almost **beside** herself with excitement.
> **Besides** them there were many people in the Observation Tower.
> John was the last **but** one. (= penúltimo)
> Nobody was in the lobby **except** Mr. Beckett.

☐ × beside

beside	l.:	junto de
	c.:	além de
besides	c.:	além de
but	c.:	além de, excepto
except	c.:	além de, excepto

6. Verbos fortes e fracos irregulares

to fly	[ai]	flew	[uː]	flown	[əu]	voar
to sit	[i]	sat	[æ]	sat	[æ]	estar sentado
to set	[e]	set	[e]	set	[e]	colocar
to cast	[ɑː]	cast	[ɑː]	cast	[ɑː]	atirar
to tell	[e]	told	[əu]	told	[əu]	contar, narrar

Exercícios 29 C

Recapitulação da passiva (lições 17 e 18)

1. Passe para a passiva:
   They spoke about the history of Manhattan. Jane listens to his words. She will remember the visit for quite some time. The Dutch first laid hold of Manhattan. Somebody made use of his knowledge of history. People took care of Tom. They will take notice of the traffic in the streets. The English called the town New York. They made this place the centre of the country.

Recapitulação do infinito dependente do complemento directo (lição 20)
2.*a*) Complete as seguintes frases com um infinito dependente do complemento directo:
Jane saw ... Jane heard ... Jane watched ... Jane felt ...

b) Passe para a passiva as frases com *saw* e *heard* utilizando o infinito dependente do sujeito.

Conversation in a Drugstore

Texto 30 A

After their visit to the Empire State Building Mr. Beckett took Jane for a meal in a drugstore. And although she already knew that a drugstore was not just a chemist's shop, it still rather surprised her, coming from England, to find a restaurant counter inside, with people sitting on tall stools having their meals. And beyond the restaurant counter there were other counters displaying cosmetics and confectionery, stationery, cigarettes, books and magazines. In one corner household equipment was to be seen, and in another there was a row of telephone booths.
«I'm surprised you still call this a drugstore», she said.
«Yes, but don't forget there still is a dispensary here, where they make up prescriptions», Mr. Beckett replied, as they took their places at the counter and gave their orders. Jane ordered eggs on toast and Mr. Beckett a «hot dog». And then they had ice-cream.
«You'll find», Mr. Beckett continued as they drank a cup of coffee after the meal, «that the American way of life differs greatly from that of the Old World. You'll notice it when you visit Americans in their own homes. Maybe there are lawns round the houses, just as in England, but there's neither a fence nor a hedge to separate one house from the other. For most Americans the word 'privacy' doesn't exist. Contacts among individuals are much more quickly made in America than east of the Atlantic. In England people keep themselves to themselves. In America they're more sociable.»
«I think you are exaggerating. Perhaps it used to be like that with us, but things have changed and it's very different now.»

«Maybe. Anyhow, in this country neighbours are friends. They will come in and help you without being asked if they hear you are in need. In the same way you are expected to help whenever it should be necessary.»

«I suppose it's a tradition which goes back to the days of the first settlers, when everybody had to depend on his neighbour.»

«You're right there. The spirit of the pioneers is still alive in the States, even in twentieth-century New York. But you'll see all that for yourself when you leave your hotel tomorrow and begin to live and work among Americans, even if it is only for some weeks.»

Notas sobre a língua inglesa e notas gramaticais

1. Particularidades gráficas do americano

Nos casos em que a grafia americana se afasta do britânico, fá-lo por simplificação e numa tentativa de aproximar a escrita da pronúncia. Aqui vamos limitar-nos às diferenças mais importantes:

a) **britânico -our** : **americano -or**
labour — labor
colour — color
favour — favor
harbour — harbor

b) **britânico -re** : **americano -er**
theatre — theater
centre — center
fibre — fiber

c) **britânico en-** : **americano in-**
endorse — indorse
enclose — inclose
enquire — inquire

d) **britânico -ence** : **americano -ense**
defence — defense
licence — license
offence — offense

e) **omissão de letras mudas**
britânico : **americano**
axe — ax
catalogue — catalog
jewellery — jewelry
programme — program
prologue — prolog

Em parte, esta grafia americana já começa a ser usada no inglês britânico

2. Diferenças nas formas e tempos

Trata-se de casos da linguagem comum que (ainda) não têm validade geral, confirmada pela escrita.
No entanto já estão muito divulgados os seguintes casos:

a) **Formação do futuro**

Também na Inglaterra está a tornar-se cada vez mais vulgar a formação do Futuro e do Condicional com *will* (em vez de *shall*) e *would* (em vez de *should*) também na 1.ª pessoa.

b) **O particípio passado de «to get»**

Só em americano se encontra o particípio passado *gotten* ['gatn] com o sentido de «recebido» em vez do britânico *got*: I've *gotten* a letter from England.

3. Emprego das conjunções

As conjunções ligam palavras (John *and* Jane), grupos de palavras (in summer *as well as* in winter) e orações (He was writing a letter *when* his friend came in).

I cannot visit you, **because** I have no time. (Causa)
John is late, **whereas** Karl arrives in time: (Adversativa)

As conjunções expressam a relação lógica entre as orações.

4. Verbos fortes e fracos irregulares

to forget	[e]	**forgot**	[ɔ]	**forgotten**	[ɔ]	esquecer(-se)
to speak	[iː]	**spoke**	[əu]	**spoken**	[əu]	falar
to catch	[æ]	**caught**	[ɔː]	**caught**	[ɔː]	apanhar
to mean	[iː]	**meant**	[e]	**meant**	[e]	ser de opinião de que
to think	[i]	**thought**	[ɔː]	**thought**	[ɔː]	pensar

Note: **to get   got   got**
 mas: **to forget   forgot   forgotten**

Exercícios 30 C

Recapitulação do particípio (lição 21) e do gerúndio (lições 22 e 23).
1. Traduza para inglês:
Depois de saírem do Empire State Building, a Jane e o sr. Beckett foram a um «drugstore». Quando a Jane entrou, um balcão comprido chamou-lhe a atenção. Viu pessoas sentadas em bancos altos a tomarem as suas refeições. Embora a Jane estivesse com muita fome, primeiro viu a loja. Podia comprar-se uma porção de coisas, como sejam artigos de papelaria, cosméticos, livros e revistas. Embora a loja não parecesse uma farmácia, era possível aviar receitas. Como a Jane e o sr. Beckett estavam cada vez com mais fome, encomendaram torradas com ovo e cachorros quentes. Depois de terminarem a refeição pediram um gelado. Enquanto comiam a sobremesa, conversaram sobre o modo de viver americano.

Chave dos Exercícios

1C

1*a*) a sister, a father, a mother, a house, a suburb, a room, a mechanic, a garage, a secretary, an office, a car, an underground, a journey, an hour

 b) [ðə] sister, father, mother, house, suburb, room, mechanic, garage, secretary, car, journey
 [ði] office, underground, hour

2*a*) You are a mechanic.
He / She is a mechanic.

b) You / We / They have a car.
He / She has a car.

c) You / We / They live in London.
He / She lives in London.

d) You are in your house.
He / She is in his / her house.
We are in our house.
They are in their house.

e) You drive to your office.
He / She drives to his / her office.
We drive to our office.
They drive to their office.

3 I am John Brown and this is my sister, Jane Brown. We live with our father and mother in a house at Wood Green, a suburb of London, and we each have a room upstairs in the house.
I am a mechanic and work at a big London garage. Jane is a secretary and works at an office in the City, the office of Johnson and Howard. The office is in Coleman Street. I am twenty-four. I have a car of my own and drive to my work. Jane is twenty-six. She takes the underground to get to her office. The journey takes half an hour.

4 is; has; at; an; has; takes; an; have

2C

1*a*) cars, cities, combs, garages, houses, journeys, landings, mothers, offices, razors, rooms, secretaries, sides, suburbs, taps, toothbrushes

 b) oral

2 John's room; the other side of the room; my father's house; the rooms of the house; my parents' house; Mother wakes Jane; Jane gives John the toothpaste; Father gives the razor to John, not to Jane; we go to the hairdresser's; they are at the Browns' (house)

3 John's room; Jane's office; the Browns' house; the parents' bathroom; the teeth of the comb; the hairdresser's shop; the side of the landing.

3C

1*a*) Mother gives me / you / him / her / us / them a cup of tea.

 b) Jane asks me / you / him / her / us / them to help her.

 c) This is your cup. It is yours.
This is his cup. It is his.
This is her cup. It is hers.

 d) You help / wash / dress yourself.
He helps / washes / dresses himself.
She helps / washes / dresses herself.
We help / wash / dress ourselves.
They help / wash / dress themselves.

2 their; He; They; him; her; it; her; Her; them; his; hers; them; them; it

165

4C

1. **Who** is a young woman of 26? Jane is a young woman of 26.
   Where is her office? Her office is in the City.
   Where (What) is Wood Green? Wood Green is a suburb of London.
   Who has a car of his own? John has a car of his own.
   Where is John's room? John's room is upstairs.
   Where is the bathroom? The bathroom is on the other side of the landing.
   Who is in the bathroom? John is in the bathroom.
   Who is already having breakfast? His parents and Jane are already having breakfast.
   What is on the table? Breakfast is on the table.
   Whose cup is this? It is John's cup.
   Whose office is in the City? Jane's office is in the City.
   Who is standing at the newspaper kiosk? Helen is standing at the newspaper kiosk.
   What is Helen reading? Helen is reading a paper.
   Which paper is she reading? She is reading the Daily Mirror.
   Who is Helen? Helen is Jane's friend.

2. Jane works with Johnson and Howard, *whose* office is in Coleman Street.
   Jane lives in Wood Green, *which* is a suburb of London.
   Jane has a brother, *whose* name is John.
   He rushes into the bathroom, *which* is on the other side of the landing.
   He takes a comb *which* is one of his father's.
   John comes into the dining-room, *which* is downstairs.
   Father, *who* has bacon and eggs, likes a big breakfast.
   Jane, *who* has a cup of coffee, does not like to eat much.
   Helen, *who* is reading her newspaper, is standing at the newspaper kiosk.
   Jane buys the Daily Express, *which* has an interesting article in it.
   Jane, *who* has another 5 stations to go, opens her paper.

5C

1.
big	– bigger	– biggest	more – most:
busy	– busier	– busiest	comfortable
early	– earlier	– earliest	delighted
easy	– easier	– easiest	elegant
gay	– gayer	– gayest	exciting
gentle	– gentler	– gentlest	famous
large	– larger	– largest	glorious
long	– longer	– longest	honest
lovely	– lovelier	– loveliest	important
pretty	– prettier	– prettiest	marvellous
rainy	– rainier	– rainiest	necessary
simple	– simpler	– simplest	splendid
thin	– thinner	– thinnest	tired
			wonderful

2*a)* early; earlier; earliest; b) interesting; more interesting; most interesting; c) good; better; best

3*a)* Jane's work is easier than Mr. Holdstock's work.
    Mr. Holdstock's work is not so (as) easy as Jane's work.
 b) Helen's coat is more elegant than Jane's coat.
    Jane's coat is not as (so) elegant as Helen's coat.
 c) The dining-room is more beautiful than John's room.
    John's room is not as (so) beautiful as the dining-room.

d) The streets of the City are more crowded than the streets of Wood Green.
   The streets of Wood Green are not as (so) crowded as the streets of the City.
e) The letter from France is more important than the letter from Liverpool.
   The letter from Liverpool is not as (so) important as the letter from France.
f) The Bank of England is more famous than the Mansion House.
   The Mansion House is not as (so) famous as the Bank of England.

4*a*) as busy as; *b*) as important as *c*) as pretty as *d*) as splendid as *e*) as gay as

5*a*) nearest; next *b*) last; last; latest *c*) farther, further

6C

1 wonderfully, gaily, prettily, comfortably, beautifully, fully, well, yearly, busily, politely, largely, wholly, in a lovely manner, necessarily, early, gently, easily, gloriously, simply

2 quickly; Almost; angrily; early; angry; very; friendly; in a friendly way; well; also; good; Today; nearest; only; unfriendly; in an unfriendly manner; almost; already

7C

1 one – two – three – four – five – six – seven – eight – nine – ten – eleven – twelve – thirteen – fourteen – fifteen – sixteen – seventeen – eighteen – nineteen – twenty – twenty-one – twenty-two – twenty-three; forty-eight – forty-nine – fifty;
ten – twenty – thirty – forty – fifty – sixty – seventy – eighty – ninety – a(one) hundred – a (one) thousand – one thousand five hundred and twenty-five
   2, 3 oral

8C

1 the first – the second – the third – the fifth – the eighth – the twelfth – the fourteenth – the twentieth – the fortieth – the (one) hundred and first; a half – a quarter – three fifths – two thirds – three quarters – a (one) tenth – a (one) twelfth – a (one) hundredth – a (one) thousandth – a (one) millionth;
lê-se: three point four; one point five; two point six oh three; (oh) point two; (oh) point oh two

2 Spring begins on March 21st (lê-se: March the twenty-first)
Summer begins on June 21st (lê-se: June the twenty-first)
Autumn begins on September 23rd (lê-se: September the twenty-third)
Winter begins on December 22nd (lê-se: December the twenty-second)
The day after Tuesday is Wednesday.
The day before Sunday is Saturday.
Today is Wednesday, November 6th, 1987.
Yesterday was Tuesday, November 5th, 1987.
I was born on February 2nd, 1972.
My mother was born on August 14th, 1942.
My father was born on January 23rd, 1939.

3 There are beautiful **houses** in this road. / This house has five **rooms**. / People keep their cars in **garages**. / Helen and Jane are **secretaries** in London. / We make lots of **journeys** together. / She's got Shakespeare's **works** in five volumes. / They've got two **basins** in their bathroom. / I bought new **toothbrushes** yesterday. / **Managers** have to work hard. / He likes bacon and **eggs** for breakfast. / The train has eight **carriages**. / Most **offices** close at five o'clock. / She doesn't like **potatoes**. / They sell **radios** and televisions here. / Henry VIII had six **wives**. / She cut the apple into two **halves**. / In autumn the trees lose their **leaves**.

9C

1. Jane Brown **was** a secretary. She **worked** with Johnson and Howard. Their office **was** near the Bank of England. John and Jane Brown **lived** in Wood Green. The house **belonged** to their parents. John **had** a room of his own. It **was** on the upstairs floor. Jane **needed** half an hour to get to her office.
2. John Brown **was** at breakfast. In front of him there **was** a cup and a saucer. John **asked** his mother for another cup of tea. She **poured** tea in his cup. John **had** some cornflakes and toast. It **was** a very quick breakfast. Father **had** some bacon and eggs. He **helped** himself to a cup of tea.
3. Jane **arrived** at Bank Station. Many people **left** the station with her. As she **was** later than *the day before* she **hurried** down the street. The streets of the City **were** crowded. In the evening they **were** almost deserted. Jane **passed** the Mansion House. She **entered** the office of Johnson and Howard.

10C

Exemplos de resposta:
see: John sees Jane every day. / John saw Jane every day.
do: I do my homework at night. / I did my homework at night.
come: her boyfriend sometimes comes to tea. / Her boyfriend sometimes came to tea.
go: They usually go to bed early. / They usually went to bed early.
sit: John usually sits here. / John usually sat here.
give: He often gives me presents. / He often gave me presents.
begin: I begin work at 9 o'clock. / I began work at 9 o'clock.
eat: We eat meat every day. / We ate meat every day.
take: She takes sugar in her tea. / She took sugar in her tea.
write: John writes to me every day. / John wrote to me every day.
find: I find London very interesting. / I found London very interesting.
choose: John chooses to watch TV. / John chose to watch TV.

11C

1.
he called	– he has called	– he had called
we met	– we have met	– we had met
you came	– you have come	– you had come
she sat	– she has sat	– she had sat
I wrote	– I have written	– I had written
you said	– you have said	– you had said
we heard	– we have heard	– we had heard
he arrived	– he has arrived	– he had arrived
we walked	– we have walked	– we had walked
they took	– they have taken	– they had taken

2. Exemplos de resposta:
   I met him last week. – I have never met him.
   I drove that car yesterday. – I haven't driven a car for years.
   She woke me at midnight. – I've just woken him.
   He went to the office at eight. – He has already gone.
   I broke my arm yesterday. – I have never broken my arm before.
   We found the keys we had lost. – I haven't found my pen yet.
   I lost my wallet last week. – I have never lost so much money before.
   I made dinner last night. – Have you ever made dinner before?
   Martin arrived at 10 o'clock last Tuesday. – Has Martin arrived yet?
   I learnt a lot in that last lesson. – I haven't learnt my vocabulary yet.
3. was; has been; walked; went; bought; have bought; arrived; was; went
4. Exemplos de resposta:
   I've **already** seen that film. / I phoned him **yesterday**. / I haven't been to the hairdresser's **this week**. / I was in London **a month ago**. / I've **just** got home.

12C

1   Exemplos de resposta:

Future:	I / we will/ shall	take / ask / know / go / catch/ walk / reach / explain / find / see
	you he / she / it will they	take / ask / know / go / catch / walk / reach / explain / find / see
Future-in--the-past	I / we should / would	take / ask / know / go / catch / walk / reach / explain / find / see
	you he / she / it would they	take / ask / know / go / catch / walk / reach / explain / find / see
Future II:	I / we shall / will	have taken / have asked / have known / have gone / have caught / have walked / have reached / have explained / have found / have seen
	you he / she / it will they	have taken / have asked / have known / have gone / have caught / have walked / have reached / have explained / have found / have seen

2   Exemplos de resposta:
He says he'll be with you in a moment. / He said he would meet me at 10 o'clock. / She tells me she'll be in London next week. / She told me she would show me some art galleries. / I hope I'll see you at the party. / I hoped you would remember. / I believe I'll win the race. / I believed I would be first.

3   Exemplos de resposta:
a) I am going to visit my uncle.
b) I'll go to the British Museum when I'm in London.
c) If I had a lot of money and time I would travel all round the world.

4   What is he going to do when he comes? / Would he like to go for a walk with us? Karl will be tired this evening. / Yesterday Jane told me (that) she would go / she would be going to the City today. / Tomorrow we are going to see / we see / we are going to visit / we visit the Houses of Parliament.

13C

1   taking, hoping, smiling, riding, putting, shutting, hopping, dying, playing, crying.

2   Exemplos de resposta:
a) I was watching the traffic. / I was standing at the corner of the road. / I was waiting for my boyfriend. / I was sitting in a café. / I was crossing the road.
b) He was reading a book. / He was playing tennis. / He was watching TV. / He was washing the car. / He was writing a letter.

3   lies; was lying; were standing; stands; goes, think

14C

1. can: capacidade psíquica Can you explain them to me?
   frase sugerida: Can you understand what he is saying?
   can: capacidade (máquinas, etc.) A film can't give you the same sense of contact… It can go anywhere, it can change the scene quickly…
   frase sugerida: The theatre can make you feel as if you know the actors.
   can: possibilidade The cheapest seats you can get in a theatre… …we can usually get tickets…
   frase sugerida: We can go to the cinema if we can't get tickets for the theatre.
   may: possibilidade… there may also be an upper part… …a large theatre may have other names… …there may be two balconies… …there may be a «gallery»…
   frase sugerida: The train may be a few minutes late.
   may: permissão May I?… May I have a look?
   frase sugerida: May I ask you a question?
   might: possibilidade… it might be difficult…
   frase sugerida: We might not get tickets.

2. | | | |
   |---|---|---|
   | he can | he may | he must |
   | he could | he might | he had to |
   | he has been able to | he has been allowed to | he has had to |
   | he had been able to | he had been allowed to | he had had to |
   | he will be able to | he will be allowed to | he will have to |
   | he will have been able to | he will have been allowed to | he will have had to |

   Frases para exemplo:
   He can speak a lot of English.
   He couldn't understand me.
   He has been able to go to America twice this year.
   He had been able to stop the car before it crashed.
   He will be able to read English soon.
   He will have been able to speak a lot of English when he was in London.
   He may be late (possibilidade).
   May he come to the cinema with us (permissão)?
   He might not come (=presente, possibilidade).
   He said he might be late (passado, possibilidade, discurso indirecto).
   He has never been allowed to have a girlfriend.
   He had never been allowed to watch the late-night film before.
   He will not be allowed to play.
   He will have been allowed to stay up late again – believe me.
   He must do more work.
   He had to work all day yesterday.
   He has had to work hard recently.
   He had to stay up all night.
   He will have to go home soon.
   He will have had to do 12 tests by the end of the year.

3. Exemplos de resposta:
   I prefer live theatre, because you feel as if you are really on stage with the actors. You can identify with the people who are acting, and their emotions are much more realistic.
   I prefer the cinema, because it takes you to places the theatre cannot go to. There are simply more possibilities on the screen than on the stage. And you never see the actor who is having a bad night.

15C

1. John is to go now.
   John was to go then. — não são possíveis outros tempos
   We are to visit Mr. Brown.
   We were to visit Mr. Brown. — não são possíveis outros tempos
   I am going to write a letter.
   I was going to write a letter. — não são possíveis outros tempos
   They are willing to help us.
   They were willing to help us.
   They have been willing to help us (before).
   They had been willing to help us.
   They will be willing to help us.

2. You were to go there. — não são possíveis outros tempos
   We were to start on our journey. — não são possíveis outros tempos
   I wanted to tell you about the House of Commons.
   I shall tell you about the House of Commons (I will tell you…).
   I had wanted to tell you about the House of Commons.

3. Exemplos de resposta:

When I was a child	I used to play football every day.
…	I used to go to the cinema every Friday.
…	I used to visit my grandmother every week.
When Karl was in London	he used to get up at 9 o'clock every day.
…	he used to go to a museum every afternoon.
…	he used to go to the City almost every day.
When John went to school	he used to work very hard.
…	he used to be tired all day long.
…	he used to get into trouble with the teachers.
When Jane was a little girl	she used to play with dolls every day.
…	she used to help mother in the kitchen.
…	she used to have lots of friends.

4. Exemplos de resposta:

   a) When I was a child — I had to visit my grandmother every week.
   … — I had to help my father in the garden every day.
   b) When Karl was in London — he was allowed to go anywhere he wanted to.
   … — he was allowed to stay out till after midnight.
   c) When John went to school — he was supposed to work very hard.
   … — he was supposed to learn French.
   d) When Jane was a little girl — she didn't have to help her mother in the kitchen.
   … — she didn't have to do much homework.

16C

1. He speaks English. — Afirmativa normal
   Does he speak English? — Interrogativa com to do
   Doesn't he speak English? — Interrogativa-negativa com to do
   Can he speak English? — Auxiliar sem to do
   He can't speak English. — Auxiliar sem to do
   Can't he speak English? — Auxiliar sem to do
   Who speaks English? — O sujeito é um pronome interrogativo – não se usa to do

   Which of you speaks English? — O pronome interrogativo faz parte do sujeito – interrogativa sem to do

   Do learn to speak English. — Imperativo enfático – com to do
   I did learn to speak English. — Forma enfática com to do

2. I visit London. / Do I visit London? / Do I not (Don't I) visit London?
You walked through the streets. / Did you walk through the streets? / Did you not (Didn't you) walk through the streets?
He goes by underground. / Does he go by underground? / Does he not (Doesn't he) go by underground?
She bought «The Times». / Did she buy «The Times»? / Did she not (Didn't she) buy «The Times»?
We have breakfast at eight. / Do we have breakfast at eight? / Do we not (Don't we) have breakfast at eight?

3. ... didn't walk ... didn't notice ... didn't attract...
... doesn't get ... isn't ... doesn't have ... doesn't like ... doesn't always read...

4. *What* is the clock tower of the House of Parliament called?
Which (tower) is the smallest tower of the Houses of Parliament?
What should everybody see?
Who admired the stained glass windows in the House of Lords?
Who did they join?
What attracted Karl's attention?
Whose seat is the Woolsack?
What has played a very important part in the history of Great Britain?
Where are the laws made for the British people?
How many members has the House of Commons?
Whose hands is the real government in?
Which party are the members of the Cabinet drawn from?
Whose chair is in front of the large table in the middle?
Who is the Queen's gilded mace placed before?
On which side of the House do the Prime Minister and the Cabinet sit?

5. Exemplos de resposta:
Where is the Daily Mirror building?
Where are nearly all the leading papers and periodicals published?
Where do you buy your papers?
How many copies do the serious papers sell a day?
What is The Times famous for?
Who do the letters to the Editor come from?

17C

1. You are given the tickets.
You were given...
You will be given...
You would be given...
You have been given...
You had been given...
You will have been given...
You would have been given...

Tom's right ankle is broken.
...was broken.
...will be broken.
...would be broken.
...has been broken.
...had been broken.
...will have been broken.
...would have been broken.

He is asked some questions.
He was asked...
He will be asked...
He would be asked...
He has been asked...
He had been asked...
He will have been asked...
He would have been asked...

He is helped by his friends.
He was helped...
He will be helped...
He would be helped...
He has been helped...
He had been helped...
He will have been helped...
He would have been helped...

The Houses of Parliament are visited by many people.
...were visited...
...will be visited...
...would be visited...

...have been visited...
...had been visited...
...will have been visited...
...would have been visited...

2. Karl was shown the Houses of Parliament (by Mr. Brown).
His guest was told many interesting things about Westminster Hall.
Karl was given a book about Charles I.
Karl was promised further trips through London (by Mr. Brown).

3. Exemplos de resposta:
We were allowed to go home early. / He was assisted by his wife. / I think I was followed. / We were helped by all our friends. / She was joined by her two sisters. / I was met at the station by Mr. Brown. / They were ordered to sit down. / He was not permitted to smoke.

18C

1. Much space is reserved for cricket.
...was reserved...
...will be reserved...
...would be reserved...
...has been reserved...
...had been reserved...
...will have been reserved...
...would have been reserved...

It is reported by the papers.
It was reported...
It will be reported...
It would be reported...
It has been reported...
It had been reported...
It will have been reported...
It would have been reported...

You are chosen for the First Eleven.
You were chosen...
You will be chosen...
You would be chosen...
You have been chosen...
You had been chosen...
You will have been chosen...
You would have been chosen...

Matches are watched by thousands of people.
...were watched...
...will be watched...
...would be watched...
...have been watched...
...had been watched...
...will have been watched...
...would have been watched...

The Oxford and Cambridge Boat Race is rowed in London.
...was rowed...
...will be rowed...
...would be rowed...
...has been rowed...
...had been rowed...
...will have been rowed...
...would have been rowed...

The Derby and the Oaks are run at Epsom.
...were run...
...will be run...
...would be run...
...have been run...
...had been run...
...will have been run...
...would have been run...

They are attended by the Queen
They were attended...
They will be attended...
They would be attended...
They have been attended...
They had been attended...
They will have been attended...
They would have been attended...

2. Exemplos de resposta:
He was found fault with. / I hate how I am always made use of. / This matter must be taken care of at once. / She was finally taken pity on. / I tried to tell them but was not taken notice of.

3 Exemplos de resposta:
   He was appointed chairman of the committee. / She was called Jane. / She was chosen to represent our school in the contest. / He is considered very unfair. / He was created Emperor of Rome. / She was crowned queen. / He was declared the winner. / He was elected mayor. / She was made president of the company. / He was proclaimed king.

19C

1
to call	to see	
to be calling	to be seeing	
to have called	to have seen	
to be called	to be seen	
to have been called	to have been seen	
to drive	to take	to visit
to be driving	to be taking	to be visiting
to have driven	to have taken	to have visited
to be driven	to be taken	to be visited
to have been driven	to have been taken	to have been visited

2 Exemplos de resposta:
a) To know you is to love you.
b) It's nice just to sit and relax in the garden. / It's wonderful to see you. / To have good weather every day would be boring. / He appears / seems to have broken his leg.
c) I'd love to come. / I want to know.
d) She asked where to go. / I know how to do it. / I can't see where to put it. / They told us what to do.
e) He's always the first to say «yes» when there's something for nothing. / Chris was the only person to bring a present. / He always has the nicest things to say. / The best thing to do is (to) forget about it.

3 Exemplos de resposta:
   I had better stop now. / I would rather be in London right now. / I had best go. / We did all we could do. / I must give Peter a ring. / He may be here soon. / She might be lonely.

4 Exemplos de resposta:
   I like to be asked before decisions are made. / There is a lot to be done. / He must have been seen by somebody. / There is nothing more to be said on the matter.

5 Exemplos de resposta:
   Go on, have a try – it doesn't matter if you miss. / I've been on the go all day. / I think I'll have a swim. / Let's have a drink. / At the moment, the Conservatives have the lead over the Labour Party. / I think I'll have a look round the shops. / ...To arrive at a conclusion: I think we ought to accept the offer. / To be open about it, I don't think it's a good idea. / To cut the matter short, let me just say that we had a great time. / To judge by his appearance, you would think that he had no money at all. / To sump up – it was a very useful meeting, and everyone learned a lot. / To tell the truth, I don't know whether to believe him or not.

20C

1
I would like you to have dinner...	Com *to do* (verbo volitivo)
She heard a clock strike...	Sem *to* (verbo sensitivo)
...and saw the school door open	Sem *to* (verbo sensitivo)
I didn't expect you to be...	Com *to* (verbo de pensamento)
Karl let Jane lead the way...	Sem *to* (depois de *let*)
I must ask you to wait...	Com *to* (verbo de expressão)
I'll tell the wine waiter to come...	Com *to* (verbo de motivação)
...let me have the bill...	Sem *to* (depois de *let*)

2. Jane saw Karl come out of the school door.
   They heard the waiter ask them what they wanted to have.
   Karl asks the waiter to bring the wine list.
   Karl watches Jane study the menu.

3. Exemplos de resposta:
   He made her pay for her own meal. / He made us take off our shoes before we went in. / She let me use her car. / They didn't let us see the photos. / He ordered us to give him our wallets. / She ordered him to leave at once.

4. Karl thought German food to be not any change for him.
   Karl found the Cheshire Cheese (to be) a very interesting place.
   Karl believed John to be a good mechanic.
   The restaurant is said to be very good.
   Jane knows Mr. Holdstock to take foreign visitors there. / Mr. Holdstock is known to take foreign visitors there.

5. Exemplos de resposta:
   a) Karl wants Jane to go for a meal with him.
      Karl would prefer Jane to take him to an English restaurant.
   b) Karl tells the waiter to bring him some wine.
      Jane doesn't expect Karl to want English food.
   c) Police believe the killer to be somewhere in the London area.
      The umpire (*árbitro de ténis*) judged the ball to be out.

6. Exemplos de resposta:
   He is said to be very wealthy.
   She was said to be the prettiest girl in town.
   They're said to have won a lot of money once.
   He is said to have been in prison.
   She is said to have been married four times.
   London is said to be one of the most interesting cities in the world.
   He is said to be a great tennis player.
   Her meals are said to be excellent.
   The food here is said to be the best in England.
   The boss is said to be going on holiday next week.

21C

1.
calling	being called	seeing	being seen
having called	having been called	having seen	having been seen
taking	being taken	visiting	being visited
having taken	having been taken	having visited	having been visited

2. Karl saw the actors **enter** the studio.
      = O Karl viu que os actores entraram no estúdio.

   Karl saw the actors **entering** the studio.
      = O Karl viu os actores a entrarem no estúdio.

   He heard Mr. Hill **explain** the studio equipment.
      = Ele deu-se conta de que o Sr. Hill explicou o equipamento do estúdio.

   He heard Mr. Hill **explaining** the studio equipment.
      = Ele ouviu o Sr. Hill a explicar o equipamento do estúdio.

   Karl watched the actors **prepare** a television play.
      = O Karl viu que os actores prepararam uma peça televisiva.
   Karl watched the actors **preparing** a television play.
      = O Karl viu os actores a prepararem uma peça televisiva.

3   Wanting to improve his English, Karl reads English papers.
Passing a newsagent's in Oxford Street, Karl bought a copy of The Times.
The Times being one of the best newspapers, Karl buys a copy every day.
Sitting down in the underground, he opened the paper.
Having found the City News, he began to read.
Though not understanding every word, he liked to read the newspaper.
The newspaper being very interesting, Karl nearly did not notice that the train was approaching Wood Green.
The train having reached the station, Karl had to get out.

22C

1   Exemplos de resposta:
There is no denying that he's right. / It's not worthwhile waiting – let's go home! / It's no good (use) complaining. / He avoids talking to me wherever possible. / I cannot help thinking I've seen her somewhere before. / We delayed leaving as long as we could. / I've done with smoking – it's a waste of money. / Have you finished making the beds yet? / She went on talking all night. / He keeps saying he's bored. / I think I'll give up trying to call her. / Leave off annoying your sister! / I don't mind walking – but this is ridiculous! / He always puts off doing his homework till the last minute. / Stop staring at that girl. / He's always complaining of having too much work to do. / I depend on Tom helping me every day. / She seems to delight in telling me bad news. / I sometimes despair of ever finishing this job. / I'm looking forward to going on holiday. / I object to being called silly. / You can't prevent him from saying things like that. / I'm relying on finding a job soon. / He succeeded in convincing me to buy the book. / I must thank him for calling. / Don't trouble about seeing me to the door. / You get accustomed to waiting in queues. / I was disappointed at not seeing the match. / I'm fond of gardening. / I'm not very good at telling lies. / She's keen on dancing. / He was proud of having won the race. / I'm sick of sitting around waiting for something to happen. / The whole house is in danger of falling down. / I was on the point of leaving when he arrived. / He attempted cooking over an open fire. / They began playing tennis two years ago. / He never ceases talking about how successful he is. / She continued talking as if I wasn't there. / I hate working on Saturdays. / He intends taking them to court. / I like reading books. / I love watching TV. / I prefer playing games to watching TV. / Do you regret telling him the news? / I remember playing here when I was a child.

2   Exemplos de resposta:
This is the place which / that / – / I know best.
She is the woman that / – / I love.
That was the best film which / that / – / I have ever seen.
Was that the first time that / – / you have been to a football match?
He told me everything that / – / I wanted to know.
All that / – / I want is a little more money.
It's you that / – / he wants to see.
That's the boy and the dog that / – / I was telling you about.
You are the man on whom I am relying.
You are the man who(m) / that / – / I am relying on.
This is the garden of wich he is so proud.
This is the garden which / that / – / he is so proud of.

3. which / that / – /; who; which / that / – /; which / that / – /; which / that /; who / that /; which; which / that / – /

23C

1. Exemplos de resposta:
   It's no use / good you (your) waiting around too.
   I cannot help him (his) feeling offended.
   I don't mind you (your) asking personal questions.
   I hate her trying to be funny.
   I don't like him (his) coming round late at night.
   He loves me (my) playing the piano.
   I prefer him (his) being here to his brother('s) being here.
   Mr. Jones regrets you (your) finding out about it.
   I remember Mrs. Smith('s) telling me that last week.

2. On / After leaving the station, Karl bought a paper. / On reaching Tower Bridge, they had a look at the Tower. / The Times is read by many people for having good leading articles. / After leaving the station, he had some money changed. / In spite of being in London for the first time, he found his way. / In the evening John and Karl wanted to return to Wood Green after having been away for hours. / In spite of having left / In spite of leaving home early, they were late for the film.

3. …fond of sports. / …prefers cricket to all other games. / …the national game… / In (the) spring… / In the summer of 1974… / The school… / …are at school. / The England of today… the England of Queen Victoria.

24C

1. John asks where the letter from Karl is.
   Mother answers (that) his letter is (there) on the table.
   John said (that) he hoped he (I, we, they) had had a good flight.
   Karl replied (that) it had been very quick.
   Mr. Brown asked what was wrong.
   Mrs. Brown answered (that) she had seen a terrible accident.
   Jane wanted to know if (whether) anyone had been hurt.
   Mrs. Brown said (that) an old man had been hit by one of the wheels.
   The guide explained (that) it was the Woolsack.
   Karl agreed that John was right.

2. …a mechanic…a secretary: / …five days a week. / …a nice meal with roast beef and wine. / … Queen of England. / …a good friend…

3. Exemplos de resposta:
   I go to the cinema once a week. / I brush my teeth twice a day. / He goes to London at least once a year. / This magazine appears four times a month. / The grapes were sixty pence a pound.

25C

1. Exemplos de resposta:
   I'll do whatever he may / might say (whatever he says).
   My dog follows me wherever I (may) go.
   You won't open that case however hard you may try.
   He'll fight any man, whoever he may be.
   He always makes time for me, though he may be tired himself.

2. Exemplos de resposta:
   a) I'll go if yo let me.
      If I see her I'll recognize her.
      He'll tell you if he knows.
   b) I'd go if you let me.
      If I saw her I'd recognize her.
      He'd tell you if he knew.

c) I would have gone if you'd (you had) let me.
If I had seen her I'd (I would) have recognized her.
He would have told you if he'd (he had) known.

3   Exemplos de resposta:
Heaven help us. / I wish I were (frequentemente: was) in England. / I wish I knew where they are. / I wish I could find my pen. / I only wish I might some day see her again.

4   Exemplos de resposta:
He had to stand on a chair to see what was happening.
I'm going to London to see the sights.
I'm taking lessons (in order) to improve my English.
We're flying to New York next week to stay with relatives there.
I'll call the restaurant (in order) to reserve a table.
He drove all the way to Manchester so that he could be with her.
He did a lot of walking in order to get to know the city better.
I've got to go to the bank (in order) to get some money out.
He loves climbing mountains so that he can be alone for a while.
I went to look at the flat so that I could see what still had to be done.

26C

1   Exemplos de resposta:
I was having a shower when the phone rang.
I've been working hard all morning.
I didn't have a shower yesterday.
I worked hard all morning.
We were watching an exciting film when the TV broke down.
I've been living in London for three years now.
We watched an exciting film on TV last night.
I lived in London for three years, then I moved back to Frankfurt.

2   Exemplos de resposta:
I **do** enjoy reading the paper at breakfast.
I'm not keen on sports, but I do enjoy cricket.
I don't spend much money on clothes, but I do like to eat well.
He doesn't smoke, but he does have a drink now and again.

27C

1   Exemplos de resposta: **ficar**:
He became very nervous, and then left the room.
He became one of the richest men in the country.
Whatever became of that old man across the road?
His face turned red.
I've grown accustomed to this part of the world.
It grew colder and colder, so we had to find somewhere to spend the night.
I get bored listening to her talking.
The children are impossible when they get tired.

deixar, mandar, fazer com que:
Let me have a look!
He wouldn't let us watch the film.
She allowed / permitted us to take as many apples as we wanted.
He made her do all the work.
I'll get my secretary to make an appointment.
I'll have someone bring it to your room at once.
I must get the car washed.
We're having the windows of our house painted at the moment.

2. Exemplos de resposta:
   Had I known you were here, I'd (I would) have come earlier.
   Had David told me the news, I'd (I would) have phoned straight away.
   Had you bought the car, you would have regretted it.
   Were I you I would (should) accept the offer.
3. Exemplos de resposta:
   Seldom have I seen such a wonderful sight.
   Rarely have I had a better meal.
   Never have I known a more wonderful place.
   In vain did she try to get out.
   Little did she know that we were watching.
   Nor did he realize what he had said.
   No sooner had we left the house than it started to rain.
   Scarcely had the match begun when the thunderstorm started.
   Hardly had we started eating when the doorbell rang.
   Not only did he steal her handbag, he also stole her watch.
4. oral

28C

1. invited; left; flew; has just arrived; has been waiting; began; discovered; were; has been, changed; drove / have driven; has been
2. Exemplos de resposta:
   After I had gone to work, the children left for school.
   Before the children left for school, I had gone to work.
   After I had warned her, she had the accident.
   Before she had the accident, I had warned her.
   After I had met David, I went to the pictures.
   Before I went to the pictures, I had met David.
   After the alarm had gone off, I got up.
   Before I got up, the alarm had gone off.
   After I had got the flowers, I wrote to thank Tom.
   Before I wrote to thank Tom, I had got the flowers.
3. is approaching; reached; came; stands; were leaving; drove up; were standing; was sitting; rang; entered; was sitting; was speaking; stopped; was looking
4. Exemplos de resposta:
   I was running to catch the bus when I suddenly slipped and fell.
   I was standing outside the bank when a man with a gun suddenly ran out.
   I was driving to work when the car broke down.
   Peter was walking down the street when suddenly there was an explosion.
   We were having lunch when Sally dropped by.
   I was just getting into the bath when the phone rang.
   I was looking out of the window when I suddenly saw a strange creature.
   She was reading a magazine when the boss walked in.
   We were in the living room when the fire broke out.
   I was crossing the road when a car suddenly appeared from nowhere.
   While I was writing letters, the children were playing in the garden.
   While I was working hard, the others were playing tennis.
   While Mr. Jones was mending his car, his wife was making dinner.
   While I was enjoying the sunshine, my brother was watching TV.
   While Chris was painting the ceiling, I was painting the walls.
   While I was studying for my exams, my friends were having a drink.
   While Peter was doing his homework, we were having lunch.
   While we were looking for them, they were looking for us.
   While I was driving to work, you were lying in bed.
   While I was making coffee, the others were sitting around doing nothing.

29C

1. The history of Manhattan was spoken about. His words are listened to (by Jane). The visit will be remembered (by her) for quite some time. Manhattan was first laid hold of by the Dutch. His knowledge of history was made use of. The traffic in the streets will be taken notice of. Tom was taken care of. The town was called New York by the English. This place was made the centre of the country.

2. Exemplos de resposta:
 a) Jane saw the dog bite the girl. / Jane heard Karl say how much he liked London. / Jane watched the boys steal the books. / Jane felt the cold water drip on her head.
 b) The dog was seen to bite the girl. / Karl was heard to say how much he liked London.

30C

1. After Jane and Mr. Beckett had left the Empire State Building, they went to a drugstore. / Having left the Empire State Building, Jane and Mr. Beckett went to a drugstore. When Jane went in (entered), a long counter attracted her attention. She saw people sitting on tall stools and eating their meals (having their meals). Though (Although) Jane was very hungry, she looked about the shop first. / In spite of being very hungry, Jane looked about the shop first (had a look about in the shop first). There were lots of (a lot of) things to buy (You could buy lots of things) – stationary, cosmetics, books and magazines. Although the shop didn't look like a chemist's, you could have prescriptions made up. / In spite of the shop('s) not looking like a chemist's, you could have prescriptions made up. / As Jane and Mr. Beckett were getting hungrier and hungrier (more and more hungry), they ordered egg on toast and hot dogs. / Getting hungrier and hungrier, Jane and Mr. Beckett ordered egg on toast and hot dogs. When they had finished their meal, they ordered ice-cream. / Having finished their meal, they ordered ice-cream. While they were having their dessert, they talked about the American way of life. / While having their dessert, they talked about the American way of life.

Vocabulário

Esta lista apresenta o vocabulário dos textos, desde que não tenha sido sistematicamente tratado nas respectivas NOTAS GRAMATICAIS ou numa lição anterior.

1

one [wʌn]	um
John [dʒɔn]	*nome masculino*
and [ænd, ən(d)]	e
Jane [dʒein]	*nome feminino*
Brown [braun]	apelido
meet John and Jane [mi:t 'dʒɔn ən 'dʒein]	apresento-lhes John e Jane
this [ðis]	este, esta
his [hiz]	o seu, a sua, os seus, as suas (dele)
sister ['sistə]	irmã
live [liv]	viver
with [wið]	com
father ['fɑ:ðə]	pai
mother ['mʌðə]	mãe
in [in]	em
house [haus]	casa
at [æt, ət]	em
Wood Green ['wud 'gri:n]	*subúrbio de Londres*
suburb ['sʌbə:b]	subúrbio
of [ɔv, əv]	de
London ['lʌndən]	Londres
they each [ðei 'i:tʃ]	cada um
have [hæv, həv]	ter
room [ru:m]	quarto
upstairs ['ʌp(ˌ)stɛəz]	em cima
mechanic [mi'kænik]	mecânico
works [wə:ks]	trabalha
big [big]	grande
garage ['gærɑ:ʒ]	garagem
secretary ['sekrətri]	secretário, -a
office ['ɔfis]	escritório
City ['siti]	*centro de Londres*
Johnson ['dʒɔnsn]	*apelido*
Howard ['hauəd]	*apelido*
Coleman Street ['kəulmən stri:t]	*rua de Londres*
twenty-four [twenti'fɔ:]	vinte e quatro
has [hæz, həz]	tem
a car of his own [ə 'kɑ:r əv his 'eun]	carro próprio
drives [draivz]	vai *(de carro)*
to [tu, tə]	para
work [wə:k]	trabalho
twenty-six ['twenti'siks]	vinte e seis
takes [teiks]	leva
underground ['ʌndəgraund]	metropolitano
to get [tə 'get]	chegar
journey ['dʒə:ni]	viagem
half an hour ['hɑ:f ən 'auə]	meia hora

2

two [tu:]	dois
getting up ['getiŋ 'ʌp]	levantar(-se)
in the morning [in ðə 'mɔ:niŋ]	de manhã
this morning [ðis 'mɔ:niŋ]	esta manhã
to wake up ['weik 'ʌp]	acordar
late [leit]	tarde
so [səu]	assim, portanto
must [mʌst, məst]	ter de
to hurry ['hʌri]	apressar-se
to rush [rʌʃ]	correr
into ['intu, 'intə]	para
bathroom ['bɑ:θrum]	casa de banho
on [ɔn]	em
other ['ʌðə]	outro, -a, etc.
side [said]	lado
landing ['lændiŋ]	patamar
to turn on ['tə:n 'ɔn]	abrir
tap [tæp]	torneira
to fill [fil]	encher

181

basin ['beisn]	lavatório
in the meantime [in ðə 'mi:ntaim]	entretanto
to shave [ʃeiv]	fazer a barba
electric [i'lektrik]	eléctrico, -a
razor ['reizə]	máquina de barbear
then [ðen]	então, depois
to wash [wɔʃ]	lavar(-se)
soap [səup]	sabonete
water ['wɔ:tə]	água
to clean [kli:n]	lavar
teeth [ti:θ]	dentes
toothbrush ['tu:θbrʌʃ]	escova de dentes
toothpaste ['tu:θpeist]	pasta para dentes
next [nekst]	a seguir
to dress [dres]	vestir-se
to start [stɑ:t]	começar
to comb [kəum]	pentear
hair [hɛə]	cabelo
he combs his hair [hi: 'kəumz hiz 'hɛə]	ele penteia o cabelo
comb [kəum]	pentear
to break [breik]	partir(-se)
too [tu:]	também, demasiado
long [lɔŋ]	comprido
soon [su:n]	em breve
to go [gəu]	ir
hairdresser ['hɛədresə]	barbeiro
after ['ɑ:ftə]	depois de
after combing his hair ['ɑ:ftə 'kəumiŋ hiz 'hɛə]	depois de pentear o cabelo
downstairs ['daun(')stɛəz]	para baixo, em baixo
breakfast ['brekfəst]	pequeno-almoço

3

three [θri:]	três
having breakfast ['hæviŋ 'brekfəst]	tomar o pequeno--almoço
to come [kʌm]	vir, ir
dining-room ['dainiŋrum]	sala de jantar
nearly ['niəli]	quase
eight o'clock ['eit ə'klɔk]	oito horas
parents ['pɛərənts]	pais
are having breakfast [ə 'hæviŋ 'brekfəst]	estão a tomar o pequeno-almoço
already [ɔ:l'redi]	já
good morning [gud 'mɔ:niŋ]	bom dia
to say ['sei]	dizer
says [sez]	diz
to sit down ['sit 'daun]	sentar-se
table ['teibl]	mesa
in front of [in 'frʌnt əv]	em frente de
there is [ðɛər 'iz]	há
empty ['empti]	vazio, -a
teacup ['ti:kʌp]	chávena de chá
cup [kʌp]	chávena
to ask [ɑ:sk]	pedir, perguntar
yes [jes]	sim
that [ðæt]	isso
that's [ðæts] = that is	isso é
to answer ['ɑ:nsə]	responder
he helps himself to [hi: 'helps him'self tə]	ele serve-se de
tea [ti:]	chá
milk [milk]	leite
sugar ['ʃugə]	açúcar
to prefer... to... [pri'fə: tə]	preferir... a...
coffee ['kɔfi]	café
what will you have? ['wɔt will ju 'hæv]	o que queres?
to eat [i:t]	comer
just [dʒʌst]	só
cornflakes ['kɔ:nfleiks]	cornflakes
toast [təust]	torrada
please [pli:z]	por favor
to like [laik]	gostar de
some [sʌm, səm]	uns
bacon ['beikən]	bacon
egg [eg]	ovo
he has some bacon [hi həz səm 'beikən]	come um pouco de bacon
first [fə:st]	primeiro
butter ['bʌtə]	manteiga
marmalade ['mɑ:məleid]	doce de laranja
grapefruit ['greipfru:t]	toranja
a cup of coffe [ə 'kʌp əv 'kɔfi]	uma chávena de café
slice [slais]	fatia
she doesn't like to [ʃi dʌznt 'laik tə]	ela não gosta
much breakfast ['mʌtʃ 'brekfəst]	muito ao pequeno--almoço

another [əˈnʌðə]	outro, -a	tennis [ˈtenis]	ténis
too look at [ˈluk ət]	olhar para	championship [ˈtʃæmpjənʃip]	campeonato
watch [wɔtʃ]	relógio	all right [ˈɔːl ˈrait]	está bem
no, thank you [ˈnəu ˈθæŋk ju]	não, obrigado	but [bʌt, bət]	mas
really [ˈriəli]	de facto	hurry [ˈhʌri]	despacha-te
now [nau]	agora	train [trein]	comboio
goodbye [gudˈbai]	adeus	is coming [iz ˈkʌmiŋ]	está a chegar
raincoat [ˈreinkəut]	gabardina	to get [get]	ir buscar, comprar
out [aut]	para fora	both [bəuθ]	ambas
too [tuː]	também (*posposto*)	down [daun]	para baixo

4

four [fɔː]	quatro	platform [ˈplætfɔːm]	plataforma
way [wei]	caminho	to arrive [əˈraiv]	chegar
station [ˈsteiʃən]	estação	carriage [ˈkæridʒ]	carruagem
only [ˈəunli]	só, apenas	the front one [ˈfrʌnt wʌn]	a da frente
five minutes walk [ˈfaiv ˈminits ˈwɔːk]	cinco minutos a pé	to think [θiŋk]	pensar, achar
from [frɔm, frəm]	de (distância)	it's [its] = it is	
the Browns [ðə ˈbraunz]	a família Brown	not [nɔt]	não
when [wen]	quando	full [ful]	cheio
to reach [riːtʃ]	chegar	to get into [ˈget intə]	entrar
to find [faind]	encontrar	won [wʌn]	ganhou
friend [frend]	amigo, -a	American [əˈmerikən]	americano, -a
Helen [ˈhelin]	*nome feminino*	girl [gəːl]	rapariga
she finds her standing [ʃi ˈfaindz hə ˈstændiŋ]	vê-a de pé	no [nəu]	não
		Australian [ɔsˈtreljən]	australiano, -a
newspaper [ˈnjuːspeipə]	jornal	this time [ˈðis ˈtaim]	desta vez
kiosk [kiˈɔsk]	quiosque	she's [ʃiːz] = she is	
reading [ˈriːdiŋ]	a ler	very [ˈveri]	muito
paper [ˈpeipə] = newspaper		good [gud]	bom, boa
hello [ˈheˈləu]	olá	while [wail]	enquanto
how are you? [hau ˈɑː ju]	como estás?	they are talking [ðei ə ˈtɔːkiŋ]	estão a conversar
I'm fine, thanks [aim ˈfain ˈθæŋks]	bem, obrigado	King's Cross [ˈkiŋz ˈkrɔs]	*estação de Londres*
I'm = I am		to get out [ˈget ˈaut]	apear-se
Daily Mirror [ˈdeili ˈmirə]	*jornal inglês*	to open [ˈəupən]	abrir
I want to get [ai ˈwɔnt tə ˈget]	quero comprar	to begin [biˈgin]	começar
Daily Express [ˈdeili iksˈpres]	*jornal inglês*	to read [riːd]	ler
today [təˈdei]	hoje	she has another five stations to go [ʃi həz əˈnʌðə ˈfaiv ˈsteiʃənz tə ˈgəu]	tem de seguir mais cinco estações
interesting [ˈintristiŋ]	interessante		
article [ˈɑːtikl]	artigo	to leave [liːv]	sair
it has...in it [it həz...in it]	traz	just [dʒʌst]	apenas
about [əˈbaut]	sobre	time [taim]	tempo
		to glance through [ˈglɑːns ˈθruː]	dar uma vista de olhos
		news [njuːz]	notícias

five [faiv]	cinco
to start work ['stɑːt 'wəːk]	começar o trabalho
half past nine ['hɑːf pɑːst 'nain]	nove e meia
Bank Station ['bæŋk 'steiʃən]	*estação de Londres*
to get off ['get 'ɔf]	apear-se
as [æz, əz]	como
to be later than [bi 'leitə ðən]	estar mais atrasada do que
yesterday ['jestədi]	ontem
down [daun]	ao longo de
Princes Street ['prinsiz striːt]	*rua de Londres*
office-worker ['ɔfiswəːkə]	empregado de escritório
going ['gəuiŋ]	dirigindo-se
street [striːt]	rua
crowded ['kraudid]	apinhado, cheio
evening ['iːvniŋ]	noitinha
almost ['ɔːlməust]	quase
deserted [diˈzəːtid]	deserto, -a, -os, -as
there are [ðɛər 'ɑː]	há
many ['meni]	muitos, -as
people ['piːpl]	pessoas
during ['djuəriŋ]	durante
rush-hours ['rʌʃauəz]	horas de ponta
to pass [pɑːs]	passar
stock exchange ['stɔk iksˈtʃeindʒ]	Bolsa
Mansion House ['mænʃən 'haus]	*sede da Câmara de Londres*
Bank of England ['bæŋk əv 'iŋglənd]	Banco da Inglaterra
finest ['fainist]	os mais belos
most famous ['məust 'feiməs]	os mais célebres
building ['bildiŋ]	edifício
next [nekst]	seguinte
to the left [tə ðə 'left]	à esquerda
nearest ['niərist]	mais próximo, -a
boss [bɔs]	chefe
Mr. = Mister ['mistə]	sr. *(+ nome)*
Holdstock ['həuldstɔk]	*apelido*
is sitting ['iz 'sitiŋ]	está sentado
desk [desk]	secretária
I'm sorry [aim 'sɔri]	faça favor de desculpar
I'm late [aim 'leit]	cheguei atrasada
a little ['litl]	um pouco
never mind ['nevə 'maind]	não faz mal
to reply [ri'plai]	responder
as...as ['æz...əz]	tão...como...
kind [kaind]	simpático
polite [pə'lait]	delicado
some [sʌm, səm]	alguns, -mas
from [frɔm, frəm]	de
Liverpool ['livəpuːl]	*cidade da Inglaterra*
Manchester ['mæntʃistə]	*cidade da Inglaterra*
Edinburgh ['edinbərə]	*capital da Escócia*
also ['ɔːlsəu]	também
France [frɑːns]	França
Germany ['dʒəːməni]	Alemanha
to give [giv]	dar
to uncover [ʌn'kʌvə]	destapar
typewriter ['taipraitə]	máquina de escrever
careful ['kɛəful]	cuidadoso, -a
was [wɔz, wəz]	era
a few [fjuː]	uns poucos, alguns
year [jəː]	ano
a few years ago [ə'fjuː 'jəːz ə'gəu]	há uns anos
still [stil]	ainda
junior typist ['dʒuːnjə 'taipist]	dactilógrafa principiante
to think it interesting ['θiŋk it 'intristiŋ]	achar interessante
to speak [spiːk]	falar
French [frentʃ]	francês
German ['dʒəːmən]	alemão
to understand [ʌndə'stænd]	compreender
Spanish ['spæniʃ]	espanhol
to be concerned with [bi kən'səːnd wið]	ocupar-se de
foreign trade ['fɔrin 'treid]	comércio externo
firm [fəːm]	firma
to know [nəu]	saber, conhecer
current ['kʌrənt]	corrente, actual
share prices ['ʃɛə, 'praisiz]	cotações

Financial Times [fai'nænʃəl 'taimz]	jornal inglês de economia	**cheque** [tʃek]	cheque
always ['ɔːlweiz]	sempre	**to change (for)** [tʃeindʒ (fə)]	trocar
latest ['leitist]	a mais recente	**bank** [bæŋk]	banco
edition [i'diʃən]	edição	**anything else** ['eniθiŋ 'els]	mais alguma coisa
to type [taip]	dactilografar	**before** [bi'fɔː]	antes de
place of work ['pleis əv 'wəːk]	local de trabalho	**to leave** [liːv]	sair de
		to (tele)phone [('teli)fəun]	telefonar

6

six [siks]	seis	**McDowell** [mək'dauəl]	*apelido escocês*
post office ['pəust 'ɔfis]	Correio	**to tell** [tel]	dizer, contar
manager ['mænidʒə]	director	**to see** [siː]	ver
Morrow ['mɔrəu]	*apelido*	**I should like to see him** [ai ʃəd 'laik tə 'siː him]	gostava de o ver
to send for ['send fə]	mandar chamar	**that** [ðæt, ðət]	que
to knock (at) ['nɔk (ət)]	bater (à porta)	**to expect** [iks'pekt]	esperar
door [dɔː]	porta	**I shall expect him** [ai ʃəl iks'pekt him]	vou esperar por ele
to call [kɔːl]	exclamar	**fifth** [fifθ]	cinco (quinto)
come in! ['kʌm 'in]	entre!	**day** [dei]	dia
to want to ['wɔnt tə]	querer	**tomorrow** [tə'mɔrəu]	amanhã
what do you want me to do? ['wɔt du ju 'wɔnt mi tə 'duː]	que deseja que eu faça?	**the day after tomorrow** [ðə 'dei 'ɑːftə tə'mɔrəu]	depois de amanhã
		at [æt, ət]	às *(horas)*
I want you to go [ai 'wɔnt ju tə 'gəu]	gostava que você fosse	**9.30 = nine thirty** ['nain 'θəːti]	nove e trinta
to buy [bai]	comprar	**short** [ʃɔːt]	pequeno, -a
stamp [stæmp]	selo	**walk** [wɔːk]	distância a pé
to need [niːd]	precisar	**to go in** ['gəu 'in]	entrar
a hundred ['hʌndrəd]	cem	**to walk** [wɔːk]	ir
20½ ['twenti ənd ə 'hɑːf]	vinte e meio	**position** [pə'ziʃən]	lugar
		counter ['kauntə]	balcão
p = penny, pence ['peni, pens]	penny, Plural: pence *(unidade monetária inglesa)*	**is waiting** [iz 'weitiŋ]	está à espera
		large [lɑːdʒ]	grande
fifty ['fifti]	cinquenta	**number** ['nʌmbə]	número
usual(ly) ['juːʒuəl(i)]	em geral	**to seem** [siːm]	parecer
		to be lucky [bi 'lʌki]	ter sorte
money order ['mʌni 'ɔːdə]	vale postal	**no** [nəu]	nenhum, -a
let's say [lets 'sei]	digamos	**clerk** [klɑːk]	empregado
to register ['redʒistə]	registar	**no one** ['nəu wʌn]	ninguém
		else [els]	mais
have these letters registered ['hæv 'ðiːz 'letəz 'redʒistəd]	registe estas cartas	**to wait** [weit]	esperar
		minute ['minit]	minuto
		much [mʌtʃ]	muito
		annoyed [ə'nɔid]	aborrecido, -a
		farther ['fɑːðə]	para a frente
		again [ə'gein]	outra vez
		angrily ['æŋgrili]	zangada

queue [kjuː]	bicha *(de pessoas)*	call [kɔːl]	chamada
her turn comes ['həː 'təːn 'kʌmz]	chega a sua vez	back [bæk]	de volta
finally ['fainəli]	finalmente	**7**	
to serve [səːv]	atender	lunch [lʌntʃ]	almoço
rather ['rɑːðə]	bastante	let's have lunch ['lets 'hæv 'lʌntʃ]	vamos almoçar
unfriendly ['ʌn'frendli]	desagradável	to finish ['finiʃ]	acabar
manner ['mænə]	maneira	typing ['taipiŋ]	dactilografar
can't you? ['kɑːnt juː] = can you not? ['kæn ju nɔt]	não (vê)?	envelope ['envələup]	envelope
notice ['nəutis]	indicação	to look up ['luk 'ʌp]	levantar os olhos
it says [it 'sez]	diz	well [wel]	bem
closed [kləuzd]	fechado	what about? ['wɔt ə'baut]	que tal?
greatly ['greitli]	extremamente	let's go ['lets 'gəu]	vamos
surprised [sə'praizd]	surpreendido, -a	nearby ['niəbai]	próximo
complete(ly) [kəm'pliːt(li)]	completamente	café ['kæfei]	café
overlooked [əuvə'lukt]	não se dar conta	food ['fuːd]	comida
to be about [bi ə'baut]	estar para	inexpensive [iniks'pensiv]	em conta
to return [ri'təːn]	regressar	corner ['kɔːnə]	canto
she remembers [ʃi ri'membəz]	ela lembra-se	to study ['stʌdi]	ler com cuidado
boyfriend ['bɔifrend]	namorado	menu ['menjuː]	ementa
he may want [hi 'mei 'wɔnt]	ele pode querer	waitress ['weitris]	empregada
possibly ['pɔsibli]	possivelmente	to come up ['kʌm 'ʌp]	aproximar-se
to go out ['gəu 'aut]	sair	to order ['ɔːdə]	encomendar
tonight [tə'nait]	hoje à noite	soup [suːp]	sopa
call-box ['kɔːlbɔks]	cabina telefónica	salad ['sæləd]	salada
to take off ['teik 'ɔf]	levantar	to ask for ['ɑːsk fə]	pedir
receiver [ri'siːvə]	auscultador	sandwich ['sænwidʒ]	sanduíche
to put into ['put 'intə]	meter	a piece of cheese ['piːs əv 'tʃiːz]	um pedaço de queijo
slot ['slɔt]	ranhura	meal [miːl]	refeição
to dial ['daiəl]	marcar o número	weekend ['wiːk'end]	fim-de-semana
297-0958 ['tuː-nain-'sevən-əu-'nain-'faiv-'eit]		plan [plæn]	plano
to hear [hiə]	ouvir	to intend to [in'tend tə]	tencionar
pay-tone ['peitəun]	sinal para pagar	up [ʌp]	acima
quick(ly) ['kwik(li)]	depressa	river ['rivə]	rio
to press [pres]	carregar	Thames [temz]	Tamisa
coin [kɔin]	moeda	as far as ['æz 'fɑːr əz]	até
connection [kə'nekʃən]	ligação	Windsor ['winzə]	*localidade perto de Londres*
through [θruː]	feita	to visit ['vizit]	visitar
		castle ['kɑːsl]	castelo
		we are expecting ['wiː ɑr iks'pektiŋ]	estamos à espera
		visitor ['vizitə]	visitante
		young [jʌn]	jovem

man [mæn]	homem	the prospect of meeting ['mi:tiŋ]	a perspectiva de encontrar
Saturday ['sætədi]	sábado	for the first time [fə ðə 'fə:st 'taim]	pela primeira vez
to stay [stei]	ficar	to please [pli:z]	agradar
for some weeks [fə səm 'wi:ks]	umas semanas	helpful ['helpful]	útil
English ['iŋgliʃ]	inglês	to decide [ti'di'said]	decidir
course [kɔ:ʃ]	curso	to write [rait]	escrever
having finished their lunch ['hæviŋ 'finiʃt ðɛə 'lʌntʃ]	quando acabaram de comer	London Tourist Board ['lʌndən 'tuərist 'bɔ:d]	Departamento de Turismo de Londres
to make out ['meik 'aut]	fazer	for [fɔ:, fə]	para
bill [bil]	conta	home adress ['həum ə'dres]	direcção de casa
out of ['aut əv]	para fora de	64, Eastern Avenue ['i:stən 'ævinju:]	Eastern Avenue, 64
bag [bæg]	mala, bolsa		
pound [paund]	libra	N. = North [nɔ:θ]	Norte
note [nəut]	nota	May [mei]	Maio
fifty-pence piece ['fifti-pens 'pi:s]	moeda de 50 pence	Grosvenor Gardens ['grəuvnə 'gɑ:dnz]	rua de Londres
several ['sevrəl]	uns poucos		
ten-pence piece ['tenpens 'pi:s]	moeda de 10 pence	SW = Southwest ['sauθ'west]	Sudoeste
all [ɔ:l]	todos, -as	SW1W ODU [']	(Número do sector do Correio)
nickel ['nikl]	níquel		
copper ['kɔpə]	cobre	Dear [diə]	Caro
halfpenny ['heipni]	meio penny	sir [sə:]	Senhor (tratamento)
quite ['kwait]	bem	could you? [kud ju]	podia
now we have ['nau wi 'hæv]	agora que temos	any ['eni]	algum, qualquer
decimal system ['desiməl 'sistim]	sistema decimal	information [infə'meiʃtən]	informação
in the pound [in ðə 'paund]	por libra	thing [θiŋ]	coisa
old [əuld]	antigo	things to see and do ['θiŋz tə 'si: ən 'du:]	coisas para ver e fazer
difficult ['difikəlt]	difícil		
most [məust]	maioria	to be of interest to [bi əv 'intrist tə]	ter interesse para
foreigner ['fɔrinə]	estrangeiro		
shilling ['ʃiliŋ]	xelim	from abroad [frəm ə'brɔ:d]	do estrangeiro
farthing ['fɑ:ðiŋ]	farthing		
to add [æd]	acrescentar	to believe [bi'li:v]	crer
half-crown ['hɑ:f 'kraun]	meia coroa	to issue ['isju:]	publicar
		leaflet ['li:flit]	folheto
sixpence ['sikspəns]	seis pence	on [ɔn]	sobre
to put [put]	pôr	subject ['sʌbdʒikt]	assunto
beside [bi'said]	ao lado de	various ['vɛəriəs]	várias
plate [pleit]	prato	language ['læŋgwidʒ]	língua
as a tip [əz ə 'tip]	de gorjeta	I should like to have ['ai ʃəd 'laik tə 'hæv]	gostaria
to pay [pei]	pagar		
desk [desk]	caixa		
		who is coming to stay with us [hu iz 'kʌmiŋ tə 'stei wið 'ʌs]	que vem passar algum tempo connosco
8			
writing ['raitiŋ]	escrever		
prospect ['prɔspekt]	perspectiva		

thanks [θæŋks]	agradeço	home [həum]	casa
in advance [in əd'vɑ:ns]	de antemão	a hard day's work ['hɑ:d 'deiz 'wə:k]	um dia de trabalho duro
attention [ə'tenʃən]	atenção	to park [pɑ:k]	estacionar
matter ['mætə]	assunto	in the road [rəud]	na rua
yours faithfully ['jɔ:z 'feiθfuli]	com os meus cumprimentos	outside ['aut'said]	lá fora
		gate [geit]	portão
formal ['fɔ:məl]	formal	garden ['gɑ:dn]	jardim
addressed to [ə'drest tə]	dirigida a	front door ['frʌnt 'dɔ:]	porta da frente
staff [stɑ:f]	pessoal	key [ki:]	chave
office ['ɔfis]	escritório	hullo ['hʌləu]	olá
to end [end]	terminar	dinner ['dinə]	jantar
to notice ['nəutis]	notar	ready ['redi]	pronto
comma ['kɔmə]	vírgula	I'm hungry [aim 'hʌŋgri]	tenho fome
phrase [freiz]	expressão		
acquaintance [ə'kweintəns]	conhecido, -a	I'll [ail] = I will	eu vou
		storey ['stɔ:ri]	andar
yours sincerely [jɔ:z sin'siəli]	com amizade	(on the) ground floor ['graund 'flɔ:]	no rés-do-chão
yours [jɔ:z]	seu, sua		
Miss [mis]	Menina	upstairs floor ['ʌpsteəz 'flɔ:]	no andar de cima
Gray [grei]	apelido		
Esq. = Esquire [is'kwaiə]	(forma muito delicada para carta)	lounge [laudʒ]	sala
		kitchen ['kitʃin]	cozinha
to supply [sə'plai]	fornecer	bedroom ['bedrum]	quarto de dormir
area ['ɛəriə]	área	window ['windəu]	janela
part ['pɑ:t]	parte	lawn [lɔ:n]	relva
England ['iŋglənd]	Inglaterra	to surround [sə'raund]	rodear
as well as [əz 'wel əz]	assim como		
		bush [buʃ]	arbusto
separate ['seprit]	separado, especial	garden seat ['gɑ:dn si:t]	cadeira de jardim
Scotland ['skɔtlənd]	Escócia	to pick up ['pik 'ʌp]	pegar em
Wales [weilz]	País de Gales		
Ireland ['aiələnd]	Irlanda	book [buk]	livro
Isle of Man ['ail əv 'mæn]	Ilha de Man	suddenly ['sʌdnli]	de repente
		voice [vɔis]	voz
travel advice ['trævəl əd'vais]	indicação para viagens	to shut [ʃʌt]	fechar
		armchair ['ɑ:m'tʃeə]	poltrona
the whole of Britain ['həul əv 'britn]	toda a Grã-Bretanha	settee [se'ti:]	sofá
		fireplace ['faiəpleis]	fogão de sala
is given [iz 'givn]	é dada	above [ə'bʌv]	por cima de
by [bai]	por	family ['fæmili]	família
British Tourist Authority ['britiʃ 'tuərist ɔ:'θɔriti]	Departamento de Turismo Britânico	photograph ['fəutəgrɑ:f]	fotografia
		clock [klɔk]	relógio de parede
St. James's St. [snt 'dʒeimziz 'stri:t]	rua de Londres	vase [vɑ:z]	vaso
		flower ['flauə]	flor
St. James [snt 'dʒeimz]	S. Jaime	flat [flæt]	apartamento
		in town [in 'taun]	na cidade
St. = Street [stri:t]	rua	for some years [fə sʌm 'jə:z]	durante uns anos

to be glad [glæd]	ficar satisfeito	supper ['sʌpə]	ceia
round [raund]	à volta de	taste [teist]	gosto
to remain [ri'mein]	ficar	in eating ['iːtiŋ]	na comida
to join [dʒɔin]	ir ter com	to vary ['vɛəri]	variar
for dinner	para jantar	to follow ['fɔləu]	seguir(-se)
[fə 'dinə]		followed by	seguido por
		course [kɔːs]	prato, iguaria

10

		fish [fiʃ]	peixe
at home [ət 'həum]	em casa	meat [miːt]	carne
best-known	mais conhecido	sweet [swiːt]	doce
['bestnəun]		often ['ɔfn]	muitas vezes
saying ['seiiŋ]	ditado, provérbio	pudding ['pudiŋ]	pudim
Englishman	inglês	fruit [fruːt]	fruta
['iŋgliʃmən]		TV ['tiː'viː]	televisão
to be fond of	gostar de	television	
[bi 'fɔnd əv]		['teliviʒən]	
to include	incluir	to watch TV	ver televisão
[in'kluːd]		[wɔtʃ]	
to do [duː]	fazer	to write [rait]	escrever
did [did]	fez	wrote [rəut]	escrevi
done [dʌn]	feito	written ['ritn]	escrito
to come [kʌm]	vir	new [njuː]	novo, -a
came [keim]	veio	colour ['kʌlə]	cor, a cores
come [kʌm]	vindo	television set	televisão a cores
to go [gəu]	ir	['teliviʒən 'set]	
went [went]	foi	could [kud, kəd]	pode, podia
gone [gɔn]	ido	to receive [ri'siːv]	receber
to sit [sit]	estar sentado	different ['difrənt]	diferente, -s
sat [sæt]	estava sentado	channel ['tʃænl]	canal
sat [sæt]	sentado	BBC ['biːbiː'siː]	televisão inglesa
everyone	toda a gente	= British	
['evriwʌn]		Broadcasting	
to give [git]	dar	Corporation	
gave [geiv]	deu	['britiʃ	
given ['givn]	dado	'brɔːdkɑːstiŋ	
to eat [iːt]	comer	kɔːpə'reiʃən]	
ate [e(i)t]	comeu	ITV ['aitiː'viː] =	televisão
eaten ['iːtn]	comido	Independent	independente
generally	em geral	Television [indi↓	
['dʒenərəli]		'pendənt	
to take [teik]	tomar	'televiʒən]	
took [tuk]	tomei	to find [faind]	encontrar
taken ['teikən]	tomado	found [faund]	encontrei
to call [kɔːl]	chamar	found [faund]	encontrado
principal	principal	detail ['diːteil]	pormenor
['prinsəpəl]		weekly ['wiːkli]	semanal (programa)
weekday ['wiːkdei]	dia de semana	to publish ['pʌbliʃ]	publicar
on weekdays	aos dias de semana	to choose [tʃuːz]	escolher
light [lait]	leve	chose [tʃəuz]	escolhi
midday ['middei]	meio-dia	chosen ['tʃəuzn]	escolhido
main [mein]	principal	to listen to ['lisn]	ouvir
may be called	pode ser chamado	pop music	música pop
['mei bi 'kɔːld]		['pɔp 'mjuːzik]	
either...or	ou...ou...	stereo ['steriəu]	estéreo
['aiðə...ɔː]		record-player	gira-discos
name [neim]	nome	['rekɔːd 'pleiə]	

to regulate (to) ['regjuleit]	sintonizar
any ['eni]	qualquer
pitch [pitʃ]	tom
own [əun]	próprio
transistor radio [træn'zistə 'reidiəu]	transistor
tape-recorder ['teipri'kɔ:də]	gravador
to record [ri'kɔ:d]	gravar
favourite ['feivərit]	preferido, -a
music ['mju:zik]	música
off the air ['ɔf ði 'ɛə]	do rádio
midnight ['midnait]	meia-noite
to go to bed ['gəu tə 'bed]	ir para a cama

11

airport ['ɛəpɔ:t]	aeroporto
to remember [ri'membə]	lembrar-se
to plane [plein]	avião
to say [sei]	dizer
said [sed]	disse
said [sed]	dito
about [ə'baut]	cerca de
sure [ʃuə]	certo, (certeza)
whether ['weðə]	se
air terminal ['ɛə 'tə:minl]	terminal aéreo
anyhow ['enihau]	de qualquer modo
he is due [dju:]	deve chegar
he won't [wəunt] = he will not	não vai
not...till [til]	não antes de
to go and meet him at ['gəu ənd 'mi:t him ət]	ir esperá-lo a
never ['nevə]	nunca
before [bi'fɔ:]	antes
to lose [lu:z]	perder
lost [lɔst]	perdi
lost [lɔst]	perdido
to get lost ['get 'lɔst]	perder-se
he may get lost if [if]	ele pode perder se
don't [dəunt] = do not ['du: 'nɔt]	não
to pick up ['pik 'ʌp]	ir buscar *(de automóvel)*
to think (of) [θiŋk]	pensar (em)
thought [θɔ:t]	pensei
thought [θɔ:t]	pensado
visit (to) ['vizit]	visita (a)
once [wʌns]	uma vez
to make [meik]	fazer
made [meid]	fiz
made [meid]	feito
experience [iks'piəriəns]	experiência
to learn [lə:n]	aprender
learnt [lə:nt]	aprendi
learnt [lə:nt]	aprendido
a lot [ə 'lɔt]	uma porção de
Heathrow ['hi:θ'rəu]	aeroporto de Londres
he makes his way (in)to [hi 'meiks hiz 'wei ('in)tə]	dirige-se
inside ['insaid]	para dentro de
TV screen ['ti:'vi: 'skri:n]	quadro de avisos
arrival [ə'raivəl]	chegada
until [ən'til]	até que
it is another ten minutes [it iz ə'nʌðə 'ten 'minits]	faltam 10 minutos
flight [flait]	voo
to pass	passar
snack-bar ['snækba:]	snack-bar
drink [driŋk]	bebida
for a cup of tea [fər ə 'kʌp əv 'ti:]	para uma chávena de chá
thirsty ['θə:sti]	com sede
to hear [hiə]	ouvir
heard [hə:d]	ouvi
heard [hə:d]	ouvido
(on the) loud-speaker ['laud-spi:kə]	(no) altifalante
exit ['eksit]	saída
to carry ['kæri]	trazer, levar
bag [bæg]	mala
to recognise ['rekəgnaiz]	reconhecer
from a photograph [frəm ə 'fəutəgra:f]	por uma foto
welcome (to) ['welkʌm tə]	bem-vindo
to hope [həup]	esperar
to let [let]	deixar
let [let]	deixei
let [let]	deixado
men [men]	homens
by the way [bai ðə 'wei]	a propósito

to want some money changed [tʃeindʒd]	querer trocar dinheiro
branch [brɑːntʃ]	sucursal
entrance ['entrəns]	entrada
hall [hɔːl]	sala
rate of exchange ['reit əv iks'tʃeindʒ]	câmbio
the same [seim]	o mesmo, -a
everywhere ['evriwɛə]	em toda a parte
I had some money changed [ai 'hæd səm 'mʌni 'tʃeindʒd]	troquei algum dinheiro
to drive off ['draiv 'ɔf]	partir

12

what are you going to do? ['wɔt ɑː ju 'gəuiŋ tə 'duː]	o que pensas fazer?
to know [nəu]	saber
knew [njuː]	soube
known [nəun]	sabido
to suggest [sə'dʒest]	sugerir
anything ['eniθiŋ]	alguma coisa
would you like to...? ['wud ju 'laik tə]	gostaria de...?
to go for a walk ['gəu fər ə 'wɔːk]	ir dar um passeio
central ['sentrəl]	centro de
Piccadilly Circus [pikə'dili 'səːkəs]	praça em Londres
to be able [ˈeibl]	poder
centre ['sentə]	centro
to catch a train ['kætʃ ə 'trein]	apanhar um comboio
to catch [kætʃ]	apanhar
caught [kɔːt]	apanhei
caught [kɔːt]	apanhado
over ['əuvə]	por
fountain ['fauntin]	fontenário
to admire [əd'maiə]	admirar
famous ['feiməs]	célebre
Eros ['iərɔs]	Eros
statue ['stætʃuː]	estátua
on top of [ɔn 'tɔp əv]	no cimo de
nothing ['nʌθiŋ]	nada
magnificent [mæg'nifisnt]	magnífico
hub [hʌb]	ponto central
fascinating ['fæsineitiŋ]	fascinante
in spite of [in 'spait əv]	apesar de
comparatively [kəm'pærətivli]	comparativamente
size [saiz]	tamanho
stream [striːm]	torrente
traffic ['træfik]	trânsito
to pour [pɔː]	desembocar
to lead [liːd]	conduzir, levar
lead [led]	conduzi
lead [led]	conduzido
dynamic [dai'næmik]	dinâmico
colourful ['kʌləful]	colorido
to explain [iks'plein]	explicar
to name [neim]	chamar
Regent Street ['riːdʒənt striːt]	rua de Londres
fashionable ['fæʃnəbl]	elegante
shopping ['ʃɔpiŋ]	comercial
shop [ʃɔp]	loja
to specialise in ['speʃəlaiz]	especializar-se em
fine [fain]	fino, belo, bom
shoe [ʃuː]	sapato
clothing ['kləuðiŋ]	vestuário
off [ɔf]	afastando-se
Shaftesbury Avenue ['ʃɑːftsbəri 'ævinjuː]	rua de Londres
in the direction of [in ðə di'rekʃən əv]	em direcção a
Soho ['səuhəu]	bairro de Londres
what about...?	O que há?
entertainment [entə'teinmənt]	divertimento
kind [kaind]	espécie
all kinds of ['ɔːl 'kaindz əv]	todas as espécies de
theatre ['θiətə]	teatro
cinema ['sinəmə]	cinema
night-club ['naitklʌb]	clube nocturno
cabaret ['kæbərei]	cabaré
restaurant ['restərənt]	restaurante
to suit [sjuːt]	agradar a
every ['evri]	todo, -a
occasion [ə'keiʒən]	ocasião

international [intəˈnæʃənl]	internacional
quarter [ˈkwɔːtə]	bairro
to suppose [səˈpəuz]	supor
exciting [ikˈsaitiŋ]	excitante
in the daytime [ˈdeitaim]	de dia
charm [tʃɑːm]	encanto
even [ˈiːvən]	mesmo
market [ˈmɑːkit]	mercado
back street [ˈbæk striːt]	transversal
to be right [bi ˈrait]	ter razão
not…until [nɔt ʌnˈtil]	senão quando
nightfall [ˈnaitfɔːl]	cair da noite
Haymarket [ˈheimɑːkit]	rua de Londres
Trafalgar Square [trəˈfælgə ˈskwɛə]	praça em Londres
bench [bentʃ]	banco
around [əˈraund]	à volta de
to watch [wɔtʃ]	observar
scores of [ˈskɔːz əv]	imensos
pigeon [ˈpidʒin]	pombo
middle [ˈmidl]	meio
Nelson's Column [ˈnelsnz ˈkɔləm]	coluna de Nelson
to rise [raiz]	erguer-se
rose [rəuz]	ergueu-se
risen [ˈrizn]	erguido
air [ɛə]	ar
behind [biˈhaind]	atrás de
National Gallery [ˈnæʃənl ˈgæləri]	Galeria Nacional
(work of) art [(ˈwəːk əv) ˈɑːt]	(obra de) arte
century [ˈsentʃəri]	século
school [skuːl]	escola
painting [ˈpeintiŋ]	pintura
modern [ˈmɔdən]	moderno, -a
sculpture [ˈskʌlptʃə]	escultura
Tate Gallery [ˈteit ˈgæləri]	Galeria Tate
to reserve [riˈzəːv]	reservar
interested in [ˈintristid in]	interessado em
to take me to [ˈteik mi tə]	levar-me a
how about…? [ˈhau əˈbaut]	E quanto?
Whitehall [ˈwaitˈhɔːl]	rua de Londres
Houses of	Casas do
Parliament [ˈhauziz əv ˈpɑːləmənt]	Parlamento
I hope so [ai ˈhəup səu]	espero que sim
unless [ʌnˈles]	a não ser que
to rain [rein]	chover
opportunity [ɔpəˈtjuːniti]	oportunidade
to promise [ˈprɔmis]	prometer
to be at a loss [bi ət ə ˈlɔs]	ficar atrapalhado
something [ˈsʌmθiŋ]	alguma coisa
writer [ˈraitə]	escritor
to be tired of [bi ˈtaiəd əv]	estar cansado de
life [laif]	vida

13

(road) accident [(ˈrəud) ˈæksidənt]	acidente de trânsito
tour of the City [ˈtuər əv ðə ˈsiti]	visita à cidade
to upset [ʌpˈset]	perturbar, afligir
what's wrong [ˈwɔts ˈrɔŋ]	O que se passa?
as [æz, əz]	quando
High Street [ˈhai striːt]	Rua principal
to see [siː], saw [sɔː], seen [siːn]	ver
terrible [ˈterəbl]	terrível
dear [diə]	querido, -a
came dashing [keim ˈdæʃiŋ]	passou
past (me) [ˈpɑːst (mi)]	por mim
tremendous [triˈmendəs]	tremendo, -a
speed [spiːd]	velocidade
driver [ˈdraivə]	condutor
at a…speed [ət ə…ˈspiːd]	a uma velocidade
reckless [ˈreklis]	descuidado
to say the least [liːst]	no mínimo
for [fɔː, fə]	porque
to ignore [igˈnɔː]	ignorar
traffic light [ˈtræfik lait]	semáforo
bus [bʌs]	autocarro
along [əˈlɔŋ]	(avançou)
at right angles	em ângulo recto

[ət 'rait 'æŋglz]
by the side of ao lado de
[bai ðə 'said əv]
Tom [tɔm] *nome masculino*
neighbour ['neibə] vizinho
boy [bɔi] rapaz
to ride [raid], **rode** guiar, conduzir
[rəud], **ridden**
['ridn]
bicycle ['baisikl] bicicleta
all three of them todos três
['ɔːl 'θriː əv ðəm]
to put on ['put 'ɔn] pisar
brake [breik] travão
to put on the travar
  brakes
to skid [skid] resvalar
to knock down derrubar
['nɔk 'daun]
poor [puə] pobre
to exclaim exclamar
[iksˈkleim]
to hurt, hurt, hurt ferir
[həːt]
right [rait] direito, -a
ankle ['æŋkl] tornozelo
to break [breik], partir
  broke [brəuk], partiu
  broken ['brəukən] partido
to lie [lai], **lay** estar deitado, jazer
[lei], **lain** [lein]
face [feis] cara
white [wait] branco, pálido
with pain de dor
[wið 'pein]
to swerve [swəːv] guinar
front [frʌnt] da frente
wheel [wiːl] roda
to mount [maunt] subir
kerb [kəːb] berma
anyone ['eniwʌn] qualquer pessoa
to stand [stænd], estar (de pé)
  stood, stood
  [stud]
to hit, hit, hit [hit] bater
to frighten ['fraitn] assustar
policeman polícia
[pəˈliːsmən]
near [niə] perto
to crowd [kraud] juntar-se uma
  multidão
to appear [əˈpiə] aparecer
licence ['laisəns] carta de condução
notebook agenda
['nəutbuk]
to search [səːtʃ] procurar

pocket ['pɔkit] bolso
to have to ter de
['hæv tə]
to confess [kənˈfes] confessar
to remark [riˈmɑːk] observar
offence [əˈfens] delito
to agree (with) concordar
[əˈgriː]
to pay [pei], **paid,** pagar
  paid [peid]
heavy ['hevi] pesado, -a
fine [fain] multa
case [keis] caso
to come up before ir *(a tribunal)*
court [kɔːt] tribunal
witness ['witnis] testemunha
to happen ['hæpən] acontecer
to interrupt interromper
[intəˈrʌpt]
ambulance ambulância
['æmbjulans]
hospital ['hɔspitl] hospital
careless ['kɛəlis] descuidado
thankful grato, -a
['θæŋkful]

14

one evening uma noite
['wʌn 'iːvniŋ]
mostly ['məustli] de preferência
stall [stɔːl] cadeira de orquestra
in the stalls [stɔːlz] na plateia
screen [skriːn] ecrã
balcony ['bælkəni] segundo balcão
I'm afraid receio
[aim əˈfreid]
expression expressão
[iksˈpreʃən]
seat [siːt] lugar
ground floor plateia *(no teatro)*
['graund 'flɔː]
there may be pode haver
[ðɛə 'mei 'biː]
upper ['ʌpə] superior
circle ['səːkl] balcão *(no teatro)*
to use [juːz] utilizar
partly ['pɑːtli] em parte
in front [in 'frʌnt] em frente
less [les] menos
expensive caro
[iksˈpensiv]
pit [pit] plateia
dress circle primeiro balcão
['dres 'səːkl]
slang [slæŋ] calão
the gods [gɔdz] geral *(no teatro)*

193

cheap [tʃiːp]	barato
box [bɔks]	camarote
or [ɔː]	ou
row [rəu]	fila
the very front rows	as primeiras filas
you know [ju 'nəu]	sabes
I'd [aid] = **I should/would**	(condicional)
it might be [it 'mait bi]	podia ser
ticket ['tikit]	bilhete
at such short notice [ət 'sʌtʃ 'ʃɔːt 'nəutis]	com tão pouca antecedência
to book [buk]	reservar
beforehand [bi'fɔːhænd]	antes
whereas [wɛər'æz]	ao passo que
box-office ['bɔksɔfis]	bilheteira
frankly ['fræŋkli]	francamente
live [laiv]	vivo
play [plei]	peça
stage [steidʒ]	palco
impressive [im'presiv]	impressionante
film [film]	filme
sense [sens]	sensação
contact ['kɔntækt]	contacto
actor ['æktə]	actor
actress ['æktris]	actriz
brother ['brʌðə]	irmão
scope [skəup]	campo de acção
wide [waid]	vasto, -a
anywhere ['eniwɛə]	em qualquer parte
scene [siːn]	cena
close-up ['kləusʌp]	grande plano
long shot ['lɔŋ ʃɔt]	cenário total
realistic [riə'listik]	realista
to smoke [sməuk]	fumar
to be allowed to [ə'laud]	ser permitido
advantage [əd'vɑːntidʒ]	vantagem
over ['əuvə]	acima
shouldn't ['ʃudnt] = **should not**	
to try [trai]	tentar
to compare [kəm'pɛə]	comparar
to understand [ʌndə'stænd], **understood,**	compreender
understood [ʌndə'stud]	
separately ['sepritli]	separadamente
different ['difrənt]	diferente
form [fɔːm]	forma
that's it ['ðæts it]	isto é
in any case [keis]	em qualquer caso
we had better stop [wi həd 'betə 'stɔp]	era melhor parar
discussion [dis'kʌʃən]	discussão
to decide [di'said]	decidir
where to go	onde ir
to have a look at [hæv ə 'luk ət]	dar uma vista de olhos
list [list]	lista
all the films showing ['ɔːl ðə 'filmz 'ʃəuiŋ]	todos os filmes exibidos
page [peidʒ]	página

15

visiting the... ['vizitiŋ ðə]	visita
guest [gest]	hóspede
to pay a visit (to) ['pei ə 'vizit]	fazer uma visita a
open to the public ['əupən tə ðə 'pʌblik]	aberto ao público
Westminster ['westminstə]	*bairro de Londres*
sight [sait]	vista
to catch sight of [kætʃ 'sait əv], **caught** [kɔːt], **caught** [kɔːt]	avistar
tall [tɔːl]	alto
tower ['tauə]	torre
bank [bæŋk]	margem
Big Ben [big 'ben]	*relógio da torre do Parlamento*
over there [əuvə 'ðɛə]	do outro lado
or rather [ɔː 'rɑːðə]	ou melhor
great [greit]	grande
bell [bel]	sino
to cross [krɔs]	atravessar
to enter ['entə]	entrar
public ['pʌblik]	público
guide [gaid]	guia
Robing Room ['rəubiŋ 'rum]	sala onde a rainha põe as vestes

rich [ritʃ]	rico	ballot ['bælət]	eleição secreta
to decorate ['dekəreit]	decorar	though [ðəu]	embora
throne [θrəun]	trono	United Kingdom [ju'naitid 'kiŋgdəm]	Reino Unido
monarch ['mɔnək]	monarca		
House of Lords ['haus əv 'lɔːdz]	Casa dos Lordes	hereditary [hi'reditəri]	hereditário, -a
splendid ['splendid]	esplêndido	monarchy ['mɔnəki]	monarquia
red [red]	vermelho		
stained glass window ['steind 'glɑːs 'windəu]	janela de vitrais	to rule [ruːl]	governar
		sovereign ['sɔvrin]	soberano
queen [kwiːn]	rainha	real ['riəl]	real
cushioned seat ['kuʃənd 'siːt]	assento estofado	government ['gʌvnmənt]	governo
in the middle of [in ðə 'midl əv]	no meio de	hand [hænd]	mão
		cabinet ['kæbinit]	gabinete, governo
to attract [ə'trækt]	atrair	responsible [ris'pɔnsəbl]	responsável
Woolsack ['wulsæk]	saco de lã		
		to draw [drɔː], drew [druː], drawn [drɔːn]	(aqui) ir buscar
Lord Chancellor ['lɔːd 'tʃɑːnsələ]	Chanceler		
to fulfil [ful'fil]	desempenhar	party ['pɑːti]	partido
Speaker ['spiːkə]	*Presidente da Câmara dos Comuns*	in power [in 'pauə]	no poder
		Conservative [kən'səːvətiv]	Conservador
wool [wul]	lã	Labour Party ['leibə]	Partido Trabalhista
to play [plei]	desempenhar		
to play a part [pɑːt]	desempenhar um papel	Social Democrat ['seuʃl 'deməkræt]	social democrata
history ['histəri]	história	several ['sevrəl]	vários
Great Britain ['greit 'britn]	Grã-Bretanha	such as ['sʌtʃ əz]	tais como
		Liberal ['libərəl]	Liberal
source [sɔːs]	fonte	Scottish ['skɔtiʃ]	escocês
country ['kʌntri]	país	nationalist ['næʃnəlist]	nacionalista
wealth [welθ]	riqueza		
economic [iːkə'nɔmik]	económico	Ulster ['ʌlstə]	Ulster
		unionist ['juːnjənist]	unionista
power ['pauə]	poder	chairman ['tʃɛəmən]	presidente
peer [piə]	Par *(do Reino)*		
lobby ['lɔbi]	sala, vestíbulo	chair [tʃɛə]	cadeira
House of Commons ['haus əv 'kɔmənz]	Casa dos Comuns	gilded ['gildid]	dourado, -a
		mace [meis]	maça, clava
to destroy [dis'trɔi]	destruir	to place [pleis]	colocar
air-raid ['ɛəreid]	ataque aéreo	symbol ['simbəl]	símbolo
to rebuild ['riː'bild], rebuilt, rebuilt ['riː'bilt]	reconstruir	Prime Minister ['praim 'ministə]	Primeiro-Ministro
		to occupy ['ɔkjupai]	ocupar
place [pleis]	lugar	opposition [ɔpə'ziʃən]	oposição
law [lɔː]	lei		
British ['britiʃ]	britânico, -a	leader ['liːdə]	chefe
nation ['neiʃən]	nação	left [left]	esquerdo, -a
about [ə'baut]	cerca de	M.P. ['em'piː] = Member of Parliament	membro do parlamento
member ['membə]	membro		
to elect [i'lekt]	eleger		

for short [fə 'ʃɔːt]	em abreviatura	either...or ['aiðə...ɔː]	ou...ou...
back [bæk]	traseiro, -a, -s	newsagent ['njuːzeidʒənt]	vendedor de jornais
to date back to [deit 'bæk tə]	datar de	stationer ['steiʃnə]	papelaria
Middle Ages ['midl 'eidʒiz]	Idade Média	as well [əz 'wel]	igualmente
to hold [heuld], held, held [held]	reunir-se	seller ['selə]	vendedor
death-sentence ['deθ'sentəns]	sentença de morte	a lot of [ə 'lɔt əv]	uma porção de
to pass sentence on ['pɑːs 'sentəns ɔn]	condenar	someone ['sʌmwʌn]	alguém
Charles I ['tʃɑːlz ðə 'fəːst]	Carlos I, rei de Inglaterra (1625-49)	here [hiə]	aqui
I'm sure [aim 'ʃuə]	tenho a certeza	a great many [ə 'greit 'meni]	imensos, -as
		to expect [iks'pekt]	supor, esperar
16		to travel ['trævl]	viajar, ir
Fleet Street ['fliːt striːt]	rua de Londres	on the underground	de metro
what have you been doing today?	que fizeste hoje?	circulation [səːkjuˈleiʃən]	circulação
to smile [smail]	sorrir	popular ['pɔpjulə]	popular
classes ['klɑːsiz]	classes, aulas	to print [print]	imprimir
St. Paul's [snt 'pɔːlz]	Catedral de S. Paulo	copy ['kɔpi]	exemplar
certain ['səːtn]	certo	four million a day	4 milhões por dia
especially [is'peʃəli]	especialmente	to sell [sel], sold, sold [səuld]	vender
because of [bi'kɔːz əv]		serious ['siəriəs]	sério, -a
black [blæk]	por causa de	Guardian ['gɑːdjən]	jornal inglês
front [frʌnt]	preto	opinion [ə'pinjən]	opinião
Daily Telegraph ['deili 'teligrɑːf]	frente	foreign ['fɔrin]	estrangeiro
close by ['kləus 'bai]	jornal inglês	news service ['njuːz 'səːvis]	serviço noticioso
right [rait]	mesmo ao pé	correspondent [kɔris'pɔndənt]	correspondente
that's right	certo	to station ['steiʃən]	colocar
away [ə'wei]	está certo	all over ['ɔːl 'əuvə]	por toda a parte
High Holborn ['hai 'həubən]	afastado	leading article ['liːdiŋ 'ɑːtikl]	artigo de fundo
Times [taimz]	rua de Londres	famous for ['feiməs fə]	célebre
Gray's Inn Road ['greiz in 'rəud]	jornal inglês	to exercise ['eksəsaiz]	exercer
journalistic [dʒəːnə'listik]	rua de Londres	influence ['influəns]	influência
world [wəːld]	jornalístico	policy ['pɔlisi]	política
leading ['liːdiŋ]		business part ['biznis pɑːt]	parte comercial
periodical [piəri'ɔdikəl]	mundo	anyone ['eniwʌn]	qualquer pessoa
to subscribe to [səb'skraib tə]	principal revista	finance [fai'næns]	finanças
to deliver [di'livə]	assinar	commerce ['kɔməːs]	comércio
to have them delivered by post ['hæv ðəm di'livəd bai 'pəust]	entregar mandar pelo correio	industry ['indəstri]	indústria
		correspondence column [kɔris'pɔndəns 'kɔləm]	sector de correspondência dos leitores

editor ['editə] — editor
institution [insti'tju:ʃən] — instituição
walk of life ['wɔ:k əv 'laif] — camadas sociais
such [sʌtʃ] — tal, tais
to laugh [lɑ:f] — rir

17
concert ['kɔnsət] — concerto
royal ['rɔiəl] — real
Albert ['ælbət] — *nome masculino*
Royal Albert Hall — *teatro de concertos em Londres*
Handel ['hændl] — Händel
programme ['prəugræm] — programa
symphony ['simfəni] — sinfonia
orchestra ['ɔ:kistrə] — orquestra
to conduct [kən'dʌkt] — dirigir
organ ['ɔ:gən] — órgão
pronounce [prə'nauns] — pronunciar
composer [kəm'pəuzə] — compositor
organist ['ɔ:gənist] — organista
I suppose so — suponho que sim
why [wai] — claro
of course [əv 'kɔ:ʃ] — é claro
to bear [bɛə] — trazer, dar à luz
  bore [bɔ:] — trouxe, deu à luz
  borne [bɔ:n] — trazido
born [bɔ:n] — nascido
for years and years [fə 'jə:z ən 'jə:z] — por muitos anos
most (of) ['məust əv] — a maioria
work [wə:k] — obra
to compose [kəm'pəuz] — compor
to forget [fə'get], **forgot** [fə'gɔt], **forgotten** [fə'gɔtn] — esquecer
to bury ['beri] — sepultar
Poet's Corner of Westminster Abbey ['pəuits 'kɔ:nər əv 'westminstər 'æbi] — Canto dos Poetas *(lugar de sepulturas de poetas célebres em Westminster)*
to quarrel ['kwɔrel] — discutir
in common — em comum

[in 'kɔmən]
prince [prins] — príncipe
(Prince) Consort ['kɔnsɔ:t] — Príncipe consorte
Queen Victoria ['kwi:n vik'tɔ:riə] — Rainha Vitória
to become [bi'kʌm], **became** [bi'keim], **become** [bi'kʌm] — ficar
monument ['mɔnjumənt] — monumento
memorial [mi'mɔ:riəl] — monumento comemorativo
Kensington ['kenziŋtən] — *bairro de Londres*
continuation [kəntinju'eiʃən] — continuação
Hyde Park ['haid 'pɑ:k] — *parque de Londres*
huge [hju:dʒ] — enorme
circular ['sə:kjulə] — circular
to face [feis] — ficar em frente
room [rum] — lugar
not only...but also [nɔt 'əunli...bət 'ɔ:lsəu] — não só...mas também...
meeting ['mi:tiŋ] — reunião, comício
boxing match ['bɔksiŋ mætʃ] — combate de boxe
ball [bɔ:l] — baile
best known ['best nəun] — mais conhecido
festival ['festəvəl] — festival
by [bai] — junto de
Waterloo Bridge ['wɔ:təlu: 'bridʒl] — *Ponte sobre o Tamisa*

18
sport(s) [spɔ:t(s)] — desporto
cricket ['krikit] — críquete
yesterday's ['jestədiz] — de ontem
test match ['test mætʃ] — desafio internacional
to reserve [ri'zə:v] — reservar
space [speis] — espaço, lugar
chief [tʃi:f] — principal
sporting ['spɔ:tiŋ] — desportivo
interest ['intrist] — interesse
full(y) ['ful(i)] — em pormenor
to report [ri'pɔ:t] — relatar
at school [ət 'sku:l] — na escola
first eleven ['fə:st i'levn] — 1.ª divisão
local ['ləukəl] — local

club [klʌb]	clube	plenty of ['plenti əv]	muitos, -as
to consider [kən'sidə]	considerar	Derby ['dɑːbi], Oaks [əuks]	corridas de cavalos
quite a good player ['kwait ə 'gud 'pleiə]	um jogador muito bom	to run [rʌn], ran [ræn], run [rʌn]	correr
to make use of [juːs]	utilizar	Epsom ['epsəm]	cidade satélite de Londres
Lord's Cricket Ground ['lɔːdz 'krikit graund]	campo de críquete de Londres	downs [daunz]	colinas
		race-meeting ['reismiːtiŋ]	corrida
ground [graund]	campo	to attend [ə'tend]	frequentar
Marylebone ['mærələbən]	bairro de Londres	to do some betting ['duː səm 'betiŋ]	apostar
Oval ['əuvəl]	nome de um campo desportivo de Londres	to place a bet ['pleis ə 'bet]	fazer uma aposta
		to laugh at [lɑːf]	rir de
south [sauθ]	sul	you'd better [juːd 'betə]	era melhor tu
I don't think so [ai 'dəunt 'θiŋk səu]	não me parece	to get to know ['get tə 'nəu]	ficar a conhecer
as a German [əz ə 'dʒəːmən]	como alemão	opposite ['ɔpəzit]	em frente
football ['futbɔːl]	futebol	bookmaker ['bukmeikə]	apostador
it's a pity [its ə 'piti]	é pena		
season ['siːzn]	temporada	**19**	
Arsenal Ground ['ɑːsinl]	campo desportivo de Londres	eastern ['iːstən]	oriental
		avenue ['ævinjuː]	avenida
game [geim]	jogo	Middlesex ['midlseks]	condado inglês
rugby ['rʌgbi]	râguebi		
event [i'vent]	acontecimento	Alfred ['ælfrid]	nome masculino
time of year ['taim əv 'jəː]	época do ano	to send [send], sent, sent [sent]	enviar
Wimbledon ['wimbldən]	cidade satélite de Londres	in English ['iŋgliʃ]	em inglês
rowing race ['rəuiŋ reis]	regata	since [sins]	visto que
		host [həust]	dono da casa
Henley ['henli]	cidade junto ao Tamisa	to correct [kə'rekt]	corrigir
to mean [miːn]	referir-se	order ['ɔːdə]	ordem
Oxford ['ɔksfəd], Cambridge ['keimbridʒ]	cidades universitárias inglesas	Dr. Samuel Johnson ['dɔktə 'sæmjuəl 'dʒɔnsn]	escritor inglês (1709-84)
		Dr. = doctor ['dɔktə]	Dr.
boat [bəut]	barco	man of letters ['mæn əv 'letəz]	erudito
race [reis]	corrida		
to row [rəu]	remar	tired ['taiəd]	cansado
round about ['raund ə'baut]	cerca de	afford [ə'fɔːd]	oferecer
Easter ['iːstə]	Páscoa	not yet [nɔt 'jet]	ainda não
between [bi'twiːn]	entre	marvellous ['mɑːvələs]	maravilhoso, -a
rowing club ['rəuiŋ klʌb]	clube de remo	to be on the go	estar a caminho
individual [indi'vidjuəl]	individual	as much as [əz 'mʌtʃ əz]	tanto quanto
oarsman ['ɔːzmən]	remador	capital ['kæpitl]	capital
horse-racing ['hɔːsreisiŋ]	corrida de cavalo	trade [treid]	comércio

whole [həul]	todo, -a	to dine [dain]	jantar
vehicle ['viːikl]	veículo	to dine out	jantar fora
crowd [kraud]	multidão	dining out ['dainiŋ]	ir jantar fora
pavement ['peivmənt]	passeio	to repay [riːˈpei]	retribuir
businessman ['biznismən]	negociante	to have a meal [miːl]	tomar uma refeição
shopper ['ʃɔpə]	comprador	lovely ['lʌvli]	encantador
tourist ['tuərist]	turista	possibility [pɔsə'biliti]	possibilidade
the day before yesterday	anteontem	Italian [i'tæljən]	italiano, -a
Sir Christopher Wren [seː ˈkristəfə 'ren]	*arquitecto inglês (1631-1723)*	Chinese ['tʃai'niːz]	chinês
		perhaps [pə'hæps]	talvez
Sir [səː]	*título de nobreza*	nationality [næʃə'næliti]	nacionalidade
architect ['ɑːkitekt]	arquitecto	change [tʃeindʒ]	mudança
to plan [plæn]	planear	to mind [maind]	importar-se
rebuilding ['riːˈbildiŋ]	reconstrução	Cheshire Cheese ['tʃəʃə tʃiːz]	*nome de um restaurante*
fire ["faiə]	fogo	tavern ['tævən]	botequim
inscription [inˈskripʃən]	inscrição	foreign ['fɔrin]	estrangeiro, -a
cathedral [kə'θiːdrəl]	catedral	to sound [saund]	parecer
to seek [siːk], sought, sought [sɔːt]	procurar	to meet [miːt], met, met [met]	encontrar
whispering ['wispəriŋ]	murmúrio	punctual ['pʌŋktjuəl]	pontual
whisper ['wispə]	murmúrio	lesson ['lesn]	lição
dome [dəum]	zimbório	to strike [straik], struck, struck [strʌk]	bater
foot [fut], feet [fiːt]	pé, pés; *(medida)*	to lead the way [liːd] led, led [led]	mostrar o caminho
stone [stəun]	pedra	Covent Garden ['kɔvənt 'gɑːdn]	*bairro de Londres*
view [vjuː]	vista		
to pack [pæk]	encher	Royal Opera House ['rɔiəl 'ɔpərə haus]	Ópera Real
warehouse ['wɛəhaus]	armazém		
dark [dɑːk]	escuro, -a	law court ['lɔː kɔːt]	tribunal
wall [wɔːl]	parede, muro	beside [biˈsaid]	ao lado
Tower ['tauə]	torre	tobacconist [təˈbækənist]	comerciante de tabaco
to go on ['gəu 'ɔn]	continuar		
Lord Mayor ['lɔːd 'mɛə]	Presidente da Câmara de Londres	narrow ['nærəu]	estreito, -a
		passageway ['pæsidʒwei]	passagem
official [əˈfiʃəl]	oficial	sign [sain]	tabuleta
residence ['rezidəns]	residência	to point to [pɔint]	indicar
pageant ['pædʒənt]	cortejo histórico	head waiter ['hed 'weitə]	chefe de mesa
to take office	tomar posse	in the name of [neim]	em nome de
traditional [trəˈdiʃenl]	tradicional	early ['əːli]	cedo
show [ʃəu]	espectáculo	to have a drink [driŋk]	tomar uma bebida
to sum up ['sʌm 'ʌp]	resumir	bar [bɑː]	bar
to enjoy [in'dʒɔi]	gozar	to cross to [krɔs]	atravessar para

199

gin [dʒin]	gin	now he is in E. he finds...	agora que está na I. acha que
tonic ['tɔnik]	água tónica	watching television ['wɔtʃiŋ 'teliviʒən]	ver televisão
draught beer ['drɑːft biə]	cerveja de barril	to help with ['help wið]	ajudar, auxiliar
to show to [ʃəu]	conduzir	service ['səːvis]	estação televisiva
wooden ['wudn]	de madeira	funds [fʌndz]	fundos, dinheiro
portrait ['pɔːtrit]	retrato	licence-fee ['laisənsfiː]	taxa de licença
sir [səː]	senhor	to finance [fai'næns]	financiar
recommend [rekə'mend]	recomendar	advertising ['ædvətaiziŋ]	anúncios
speciality ['speʃi'æliti]	especialidade	possible ['pɔsəbl]	possível
steak [steik]	bife	studio ['stjuːdiəu]	estúdio
kidney [kidni]	rim	party ['pɑːti]	grupo
pudding ['pudiŋ]	pudim, pastel	George [dʒɔːdʒ]	nome masculino
roast beef ['rəust 'biːf]	vaca assada	Hill [hil]	apelido
Yorkshire pudding ['jɔːkʃə]	iguaria inglesa	he happens to work ['hæpənz]	por acaso trabalha
across [ə'krɔs]	para a frente	to appoint [ə'pɔint]	combinar
melon ['melən]	melão	Shepherd's Bush ['ʃepədz buʃ]	bairro de Londres
wine list ['wain list]	lista de vinhos	to find one's way	encontrar o caminho
wine [wain]	vinho	White City ['wait 'siti]	bairro de Londres
waiter ['weitə]	empregado	to approach [ə'prəutʃ]	aproximar-se
anything to follow?	e a seguir?	shape [ʃeip]	forma
cheese [tʃiːz]	queijo	court [kɔːt]	pátio
let me see [let mi 'siː]	deixa-me ver	receptionist [ri'sepʃənist]	recepcionista
pancake ['pænkeik]	panqueca	to show round ['ʃəu 'raund]	guiar
apple ['æpl]	maçã	to prepare [pri'pɛə]	preparar
tart [tɑːt]	tarte	broadcasting ['brɔːdkɑːstiŋ]	radiodifundir
fresh [freʃ]	fresco, -a	to take place ['teik 'pleis]	ter lugar
strawberry ['strɔːbəri]	morango	to construct [kən'strʌkt]	construir
cream [kriːm]	nata	sound [saund]	som
both (of us) ['bəuθ (əv ʌs)]	ambos, -as	keep [kiːp], kept, kept [kept]	manter
enjoyable [in'dʒɔiəbl]	agradável	to keep out	afastar
afterwards ['ɑːftəwədz]	depois	to light [lait], lit, lit [lit]	iluminar
to bring [briŋ], brought, brought [brɔːt]	trazer trazer	artificial [ɑːti'fiʃəl]	artificial
21		light [lait]	luz
radio [reidiəu]	rádio	ventilator ['ventileitə]	ventilador
programme ['prəugræm]	programa	corridor ['kɔridɔː]	corredor
English by Radio	lições de inglês pela rádio	camera ['kæmərə]	câmara
because [bi'kɔz]	porque		
to improve [im'pruːv]	melhorar		
knowledge ['nɔlidʒ]	conhecimento		

microphone ['maikrəfəun]	microfone
signal ['signl]	sinal
to pass [pɑːs]	passar
to broadcast ['brɔːdkɑːst], broadcast(ed), broadcast(ed)	radiodifundir
transmitter [træns'mitə]	transmissor
production [prə'dʌkʃən]	produção
light [lait]	leve
to impress [im'pres]	impressionar
scenery ['siːnəri]	cenário
arc-light ['ɑːklait]	arco voltaico
equipment [i'kwipmənt]	equipamento
library ['laibrəri]	biblioteca
to thank [θæŋk]	agradecer
kindness ['kaindnis]	gentileza
working ['wəːkiŋ]	funcionamento
to come on [kʌm]	chegar
to make one's way [wʌnz 'wei]	regressar

22

natural ['nætʃrəl]	natural
chemist ['kemist]	farmácia
confectioner [kən'fekʃnə]	pastelaria
florist ['flɔːrist]	florista
to show [ʃəu], showed [ʃəud], shown [ʃəun]	mostrar
to burst out laugh-Ing [bəːst 'aut 'lɑːfiŋ], burst, burst [bəːst]	desatar a rir
customs ['kʌstəmz] Pl.	alfândega
come on [kʌm 'ɔn]	olha lá
to stop [stɔp]	acabar
to joke [dʒəuk]	brincar
to start [stɑːt]	começar
Carnaby Street ['kɑːnəbi striːt]	ruas de Londres com lojas para jovens
King's Road ['kiŋz rəud]	
for [fɔː, fə]	para
Burberry ['bəːbəri]	nome de uma firma
item ['aitəm]	coisa
suit [sjuːt]	fato
to make to order ['meik tə 'ɔːdə]	fazer por encomenda
men's tailor ['menz teilə]	alfaiate
clothes [kləuðz]	roupas
record ['rekɔːd]	disco
Charing Cross Road ['tʃɛəriŋ krɔs 'rəud]	rua de Londres
Selfridge ['selfridʒ]	armazém de Londres
assistant [ə'sistənt]	empregado
gentlemen ['dʒentlmən], Sg. gentleman ['dʒentlmən]	cavalheiros
this way ['ðis wei]	por aqui
rear ['riə]	fundo
it doesn't matter ['mætə]	não faz mal
to measure ['meʒə]	medir
to fit [fit]	ficar bem
special ['speʃəl]	especial
in mind [in 'maind]	na ideia
light [lait]	claro, -a
stock [stɔk]	stock
to select [si'lekt]	escolher
to try on [trai 'ɔn]	experimentar
eventually [i'ventʃuəli]	finalmente
exact [ig'zækt]	exacto, -a
shade [ʃeid]	cor, tom
shoulder ['ʃəuldə]	ombro
sleeve [sliːv]	manga
length [leŋθ]	comprimento
however [hau'evə]	contudo
to shorten ['ʃɔːtn]	encurtar
measurement ['meʒəmənt]	medida
to mark [mɑːk]	marcar
according [ə'kɔːdiŋ]	de acordo
to satisfay ['sætisfai]	satisfazer
together [tə'geðə]	juntos
to head for [hed]	dirigir-se a

23

east [iːst]	leste
East End [iːst 'end]	zona oriental
Petticoat Lane ['petikəut 'lein]	rua de Londres
they say	dizem
to make money ['mʌni]	ganhar dinheiro
west [west]	oeste

to spend [spend], spent, spent [spent]	gastar *(dinheiro)*, passar *(tempo)*	landmark ['lændmɑːk]	emblema
to mean [miːn], meant, meant [ment]	significar	edifice ['edifis]	edifício
		fortress ['fɔːtris]	fortaleza
		prison ['prizn]	prisão
peculiar [pi'kjuːljə]	peculiar	museum ['mjuːziəm]	museu
what sort of [ʃɔːt]	que espécie de	port [pɔːt]	porto
Liverpool Street Station ['livəpuːl]	estação de Londres	eastwards ['iːstwədz]	para leste
to direct [di'rekt]	mostrar o caminho	mile [mail]	milha
to worry ['wʌri]	preocupar-se	for miles [mailz]	várias milhas
to push [puʃ]	empurrar	crane [krein]	guindaste
dense [dens]	denso, -a	down the river ['daun ðə 'rivə]	pelo rio abaixo
Middlesex Street ['midlseks]	rua de Londres	dock [dɔk]	doca
to realise ['riəlaiz]	notar	Tilbury ['tilbəri]	cidade junto ao Tamisa
namely ['neimli]	nomeadamente	activity [æk'tiviti]	actividade
stall [stɔːl]	barraca	workday ['wəːkdei]	dia da semana
stand [stænd]	posto de venda	hive [haiv]	colmeia
dealer ['diːlə]	comerciante	industry ['indəstri]	indústria
to shout [ʃaut]	gritar	to take a boat trip ['bəut trip]	dar um passeio de barco
ware [wɛə]	mercadoria		
to offer ['ɔfə]	oferecer	Greenwich ['grinidʒ]	cidade antes de Londres
for sale [seil]	para venda		
everything ['evriθiŋ]	tudo	observatory [əb'zəːvətri]	observatório
imaginable [i'mædʒinəbl]	imaginável	**24**	
endless ['endlis]	infinito, -a	boat [bəut]	barco
variety [və'raiəti]	variedade	relaxing [ri'læksiŋ]	relaxante
to extend [iks'tend]	estender-se	to feel like walking ['fiːl laik 'wɔːkiŋ], felt, felt [felt]	apetecer um passeio
toilet ['tɔilit]	cosmética		
jewellery ['dʒuːəlri]	joalharia	any further ['eni 'fəːðə]	mais longe
travel ['trævl]	viagem		
goods [gudz]	mercadorias	at the moment ['məumənt]	de momento
household pet ['haushəuld pet]	animal doméstico		
		riverboat ['rivəbəut]	barco fluvial
secondhand ['sekəndhænd]	em segunda mão	to tire ['taiə]	fatigar
		top deck ['tɔp 'dek]	convés superior
junk [dʒʌŋk]	velharias	breeze [briːz]	brisa
it is well worth [wəːθ]	vale a pena	to refresh [ri'freʃ]	refrescar
		ship [ʃip]	navio
eloquence ['eləukwəns]	eloquência	entrance ['entrəns]	entrada
mouth [mauθ]	boca	commentary ['kɔmentəri]	comentário
constant ['kɔnstənt]	constante	Pilgrim Fathers ['pilgrim 'fɑːðəz]	*primeiros puritanos que emigraram para a América*
motion ['məuʃən]	movimento		
customer ['kʌstəmə]	cliente		
district ['distrikt]	distrito	to set sail for [set 'seil fə]	fazer-se à vela
to depress [di'pres]	deprimir		
slum [slʌm]	bairro de lata	America [ə'merikə]	América
dirty ['dəːti]	sujo, -a	Mayflower ['meiflauə]	*nome de um barco*

inn [in]	estalagem	at last [ət 'lɑːst]	por fim
Rotherhithe ['rɔðəhaið]	*bairro de Londres*	**to be thirsty** ['θəːsti]	ter sede
site [sait]	sítio	pub [pʌb]	bar
Deptford ['detfəd]	*bairro de Londres*		
naval ['neivəl]	naval		**25**
dockyard ['dɔkjɑːd]	estaleiro	**sight** [sait]	coisa interessante
Sir Francis Drake ['frɑːnsis 'dreik]	*navegador inglês (1540?-1596)*	**surroundings** [sə'raundiŋz]	arredores
to knight [nait]	armar cavaleiro	**uncle** ['ʌŋkl]	tio
Russian ['rʌʃən]	russo	**county** ['kaunti]	condado
emperor ['empərə]	imperador	**within easy reach of** [wi'ðin 'iːzi 'riːtʃ]	de fácil alcance
Peter ['piːtə]	*nome masculino*		
shipbuilding ['ʃipbildiŋ]	construção naval	**to bring to life** ['briŋ tə 'laif]	ilustrar
college ['kɔlidʒ]	faculdade	**Brian** ['braiən]	*nome masculino*
hill [hil]	colina	**to illustrate** ['iləstreit]	ilustrar
Greenwich time ['grinidʒ taim]	hora de Greenwich	**talk** [tɔːk]	palestra
hour ['auə]	hora	**coloured** ['kʌləd]	colorido, -a
in an hour's time	dentro de uma hora	**slide** [slaid]	diapositivo
line [lain]	linha	**ancient** ['einʃənt]	antigo
meridian [mə'ridiən]	meridiano	**borough** ['bʌrə]	município
to climb [klaim]	trepar	**Berkshire** ['bɑːkʃiə]	*condado inglês*
at the top [tɔp]	no cimo	**since** [sins]	desde
to take a photograph ['fəutəgrɑːf]	tirar uma foto	**William the Conqueror** ['wiljəm ðə 'kɔŋkərə]	Guilherme, *o Conquistador*
western ['westən]	ocidental	**to ascend** [ə'send]	subir
hemisphere ['hemisfiə]	hemisfério	**to overlook** [əuvə'luk]	abranger com a vista
unfortunately [ʌn'fɔːtʃnitli]	infelizmente	**valley** ['væli]	vale
historic [his'tɔrik]	histórico	**to be in residence**	estar presente
telescope ['teliskəup]	telescópio	**lover** ['lʌvə]	amante
loud [laud]	alto, sonoro	**connoisseur** [kɔnə'səː]	conhecedor
distance ['distəns]	distância	**architecture** ['ɑːkitektʃə]	arquitectura
like ['laik]	gostar	**St. George** [snt 'dʒɔːdʒ]	S. Jorge
to be free to ['friː]	ter liberdade de	**chapel** ['tʃæpəl]	capela
to speak [spiːk], **spoke** [spəuk], **spoken** [spəukən]	falar	**burial-place** ['beriəlpleis]	sepultura
under ['ʌndə]	debaixo de	**perfect** ['pəːfikt]	perfeito, -a
sun ['sʌn]	sol	**example** [ig'zɑːmpl]	exemplo
to fascinate ['fæsineit]	fascinar	**Perpendicular style** [pəːpən'dikjulə 'stail]	gótico tardio inglês
wildness ['waildnis]	ardor		
speech ['spiːtʃ]	discurso	**worthwhile** ['wəːθ'wail]	valer a pena
good-humoured ['gud'hjuːməd]	bem-humorado	**state apartment** ['steit ə'pɑːtmənt]	aposento do Estado
tolerance ['tɔlərəns]	tolerância		
audience ['ɔːdjəns]	público		

to contain [kən'tein]	conter
superb [sju'pə:b]	magnífico, -a
collection [kə'lekʃən]	colecção
picture ['piktʃə]	quadro
terrace ['terəs]	terraço
round [raund]	redondo, -a
across [ə'krɔs]	do outro lado
northern ['nɔ:ðən]	setentrional
Eton College ['i:tn kɔlidʒ]	célebre escola inglesa
public school ['pʌblik 'sku:l]	escola particular
to found [faund]	fundar
king [kiŋ]	rei
Henry VI ['henri ðə 'siksθ]	Henrique VI
to erect [i'rekt]	erguer
then [ðən]	então
to preserve [pri'zə:v]	preservar
yard [jɑ:d]	pátio
rewarding [ri'wɔ:diŋ]	compensador, -a
although [ɔ:l'ðou]	embora
no longer [nəu 'lɔŋgə]	já não
to wear [wɛə], wore [wɔ:], worn [wɔ:n]	usar *(roupa)*
top-hat ['tɔp'hæt]	chapéu alto
jacket ['dʒækit]	casaco
tailcoat ['teilkəut]	casaca
politician ['pɔli'tiʃən]	político
diplomat ['diplǝmæt]	diplomata
Old Etonian [i:'təunjən]	antigos estudantes de Eton
palace ['pælis]	palácio
Hampton Court ['hæmptən 'kɔ:t]	*nome de um castelo*
cardinal ['kɑ:dinl]	cardeal
Wolsey ['wulzi]	*apelido*
to take over	continuar
fall [fɔ:l]	queda
to haunt [hɔ:nt]	assombrar
vine [vain]	vinha
maze [meiz]	labirinto
meadow ['medəu]	prado
Runnymede ['rʌnimi:d]	*topónimo*
Magna C(h)arta ['mægnə 'kɑ:tə]	Magna Carta
to sign [sain]	assinar
north [nɔ:θ]	ao norte de
St. Alban's [snt 'ɔ:lbənz]	*cidade inglesa*
Hertfordshire ['hɑ:fədʃiə]	*condado inglês*
Verulamium [veru'leimjəm]	*topónimo latino*
important [im'pɔtənt]	importante
Roman ['rəumən]	romano, -a
present ['preznt]	actual
Norman ['nɔ:mən]	normando, -a
church [tʃ:tʃ]	igreja
tile [tail]	telha
brick [brik]	tijolo
close to [kləus]	perto de
Hatfield House ['hætfi:ld]	*solar inglês*
stately ['steitli]	magnífico, -a
Cecil ['sesl]	*apelido*
childhood ['tʃaildhud]	infância
Elizabeth [i'lizəbəθ]	*nome feminino*

26

section ['sekʃən]	secção
few [fju:]	poucos, -as
in the world [we:ld]	do mundo
drama ['drɑ:mə]	drama, peça de teatro
in the field of [fi:ld]	no campo de
genius ['dʒi:njəs]	génio
Shakespeare ['ʃeikspiə]	poeta inglês *(1546-1616)*
to prevail [pri'veil]	prevalecer
all these centuries ['sentʃuriz]	nos últimos séculos
decade ['dekeid]	década
to produce [prə'dju:s]	produzir
excellent ['eksələnt]	excelente
playwright ['pleirait]	dramaturgo
human ['hju:mən]	humano, -a
insight ['insait]	compreensão
dramatic [drə'mætik]	dramático, -a
skill [skil]	perícia
poet ['pəuit]	poeta
unsurpassed ['ʌnsə'pɑ:st]	inultrapassado
to owe [əu]	dever

to retire [ri'taiə]	afastar-se
in the countryside ['kʌntrisaid]	no campo
to leave behind ['liːv bi'haind], **left, left** [left]	deixar
to develop [di'veləp]	desenvolver(-se)
thirst (for) [θəːst]	sede de
wonder ['wʌndə]	maravilha
what wonder then	não admira pois
as many as [əz 'meni əz]	nada menos que
quality ['kwɔliti]	qualidade
central ['sentrəl]	central
to undergo [ʌndə'gəu], **underwent** [ʌndə'went], **undergone** [ʌndə'gɔn]	sofrer
reconstruction ['riːkən'strʌkʃən]	reconstrução
recent ['riːsnt]	recente
to carry out ['kæri 'aut]	realizar
Drury Lane ['druəri 'lein]	rua de Londres
present-day ['preznt'dei]	actual
original [ə'ridʒənl]	original
nowadays ['nauədeiz]	hoje em dia
large-scale ['lɑːdʒ'skeil]	em grande escala
musical ['mjuːzikəl]	musical
to perform [pə'fɔːm]	representar
vast [vɑːst]	vasto, -a
in fact [in 'fækt]	de facto
to create [kri'eit]	criar
sensation [sen'seiʃən]	sensação
impresario [impre'sɑːriəu]	empresário
tradition [trə'diʃən]	tradição
straight [streit]	convencional
to share [ʃɛə]	partilhar
reputation [repju'teiʃən]	reputação
elaborate [i'læbərit]	cuidadosamente preparados
majesty ['mædʒisti]	majestade
to be situated ['sitjueitid]	ficar situado
sometimes ['sʌmtaimz]	às vezes
«Theatreland» ['θiətəlænd]	terra do teatro
to house [hauz]	abrigar
first-class ['fəːst'klɑːs]	de primeira classe
repertory ['repətəri]	repertório
play [plei]	peça de teatro
Shakespearean [ʃeik'spiəriən]	de Shakespeare
classical ['klæsikəl]	clássico, -a
for instance [fər 'instəns]	por exemplo
admirer [əd'maiərə]	admirador
grand opera ['grænd 'ɔpərə]	grande ópera
ballet ['bælei]	ballet
Coliseum [kɔli'siəm]	coliseu
Sadler's Wells ['sædləz 'welz]	nome de um teatro
Palladium [pə'leidjəm]	Paládio
variety [və'raiəti]	variedade
revue [ri'vjuː]	revista
to concentrate on ['kɔnsəntreit]	concentrar-se em
experimental [eksperi'mentl]	experimental
facility [fə'siliti]	facilidade
dead [ded]	morto, -a

27

pleasant ['pleznt]	agradável
farewell [fɛə'wel]	despedida
to grow fond of [grəu 'fɔnd]	começar a gostar
extreme [iks'triːm]	extremo, -a
thanks [θæŋks]	graças a
happy ['hæpi]	feliz
sense of humour ['sens əv 'hjuːmə]	sentido de humor
joke [dʒəuk]	anedota
enough [i'nʌf]	bastante
good enough to	suficientemente bom para
to cross into [krɔs]	atravessar
(Red) Indian [('red) 'indjən]	índio
territory ['teritəri]	território
deep [diːp]	profundamente
in thought [θɔːt]	em pensamentos
pipe of peace ['paip əv 'piːs]	cachimbo da paz

to lift [lift]	levantar	sky [skai]	céu
to greet [gri:t]	saudar	harbour ['hɑ:bə]	porto
how [hau]	1. saudação índia	liberty ['libəti]	liberdade
	2. como	newcomer ['nju:'kʌmə]	recém-chegado
to prove [pru:v]	comprovar		
I might as well	posso experimentar	torch [tɔ:tʃ]	facho
prompt [prɔmpt]	pronto, imediato	ocean ['əuʃən]	oceano
reply [ri'plai]	réplica	to land [lænd]	aterrar
to baffle ['bæfl]	ficar perplexo	Kennedy Airport ['kenidi 'ɛəpɔ:t]	aeroporto de Nova Iorque
word [wə:d]	palavra		
whereupon [wɛərə'pɔn]	ao que	to hail [heil]	fazer sinal, chamar
		taxi ['tæksi]	táxi
fried [fraid]	estrelados	hotel [həu'tel]	hotel
fried eggs	ovos estrelados	(tele)phone [('teli)fəun]	telefone
double ['dʌbl]	duplo, -a		
meaning ['mi:niŋ]	significado	to ring [riŋ], rang [ræŋ], rung [rʌŋ]	tocar
story ['stɔ:ri]	história		
obvious ['ɔbviəs]	óbvio	Beckett ['bekit]	apelido
a great deal [di:l]	grande quantidade	in a minute ['minit]	num minuto
all the more ['ɔ:l ðə mɔ:]	tanto mais	Bill [bil]	nome masculino
		agent ['eidʒənt]	agente
determined [di'tə:mind]	resolvido	to shake hands [ʃeik 'hændz], shook [ʃuk], shaken ['ʃeikən]	apertar a mão
to drink (to) [driŋk]	beber		
to raise [reiz]	erguer		
glass [glɑ:s]	copo	I thank you (so much) [θæŋk]	muito obrigado
		offer ['ɔfə]	oferta
28		don't mention it ['dəunt 'menʃən it]	de nada
impression [im'preʃən]	impressão		
		to get going /A	ir andando
New York ['nju: 'jɔ:k]	Nova Iorque	to drive [draiv], drove [drəuv], driven ['drivn]	guiar, conduzir
departure [di'pɑ:tʃə]	partida		
to invite [in'vait]	convidar	rocky ['rɔki]	rochoso, -a
week [wi:k]	semana	gorge [gɔ:dʒ]	garganta
to be beside oneself ['bi: bi'said]	ficar fora de si	to tower ['tauə]	elevar-se
		than [ðæn, ðən]	do que
excitement [ik'saitmənt]	excitação	Henry ['henri]	nome masculino
		explorer [iks'plɔ:rə]	explorador
to fly [flai], flew [flu:], flown [fləun]	voar	passage ['pæsidʒ]	passagem
		Asia ['eiʃə]	Ásia
Atlantic [ət'læntik]	Atlântico	to discover [dis'kʌvə]	descobrir
distant ['distənt]	distante		
outline ['autlain]	silhueta	to sail [seil]	velejar
skyscraper ['skaiskreipə]	arranha-céus	settler ['setlə]	colono
		Dutch [dʌtʃ]	holandês
Manhattan [mæn'hætən]	parte central de Nova Iorque	colonist ['kɔlənist]	colonizador
		to buy [bai], bought, bought [bɔ:t]	comprar
island ['ailənd]	ilha		
Hudson ['hʌdsn]	nome de um rio		
to reach [ri:tʃ]	atingir	settlement ['setlmənt]	colónia
high up ['hai 'ʌp]	lá no alto	New Amsterdam ['æmstə'dæm]	antigo nome de Nova Iorque

to capture ['kæptʃə]	conquistar	blue [bluː]	azul
to change (to) [tʃeindʒ]	mudar para	to move [muːv]	mover(-se)
to stop [stɔp]	parar	slow [sləu]	lento, -a
Empire State Building ['empaiə 'steit 'bildiŋ]	arranha-céus de Nova Iorque	towards [tə'wɔːdz]	em direcção a
high [hai]	alto, -a	clear [kliə]	claro, -a
innumerable [i'njuːmərəbl]	inúmero	direction [di'rekʃən]	direcção
to vanish ['væniʃ]	desaparecer	forest ['fɔrist]	floresta
cloud [klaud]	nuvem	Greater New York	Grande Nova Iorque
indeed [in'diːd]	na verdade	far and wide ['faːr ənd 'waid]	a perder de vista
not…any more	já não	radius ['reidjəs]	raio
center ['sentər] = Inglês Americano para centre	centro	wide [waid]	largo
	nome próprio	inhabitant [in'hæbitənt]	habitante
Sears [siəz]	Chicago	population [pɔpju'leiʃən]	população
Chicago [ʃi'kaːgəu]	abrigar	quarter ['kwɔːtə]	bairro
to house [hauz]	elevador	melting-pot ['meltiŋpɔt]	cadinho
lift [lift]	observação	United Nations [juː'naitid 'neiʃənz]	Nações Unidas
observation [ɔbsə'veiʃən]	elevador	systematic(ally) [sisti'mætik(əli)]	sistematicamente
elevator ['eliveitə] IA	Outono	to build [bild], built, built [bilt]	construir
autumn ['ɔːtəm]	Outono	system ['sistim]	sistema
fall [fɔːl] IA	passeio	block [blɔk]	bloco
sidewalk ['saidwɔːk] IA	automóvel	regular ['regjulə]	regular
motor-car ['məutəkaː]	automóvel	pattern ['pætən]	desenho
automobile ['ɔːtəməubiːl]	parque de estacionamento	square [skwɛə]	quadrado
car park ['kaː paːk]		road [rəud]	rua
parking place ['paːkiŋ] IA	parque de estacionamento	to run [rʌn], ran [ræn], run [rʌn]	ir, estender-se
to amount to [ə'maunt]	atingir	end [end]	fim, final
to differ ['difə]	diferir	as a rule [ruːl]	em regra
way [wei]	modo	simple ['simpl]	simples
mass [mæs]	massa	to number ['nʌmbə]	numerar
motionless ['məuʃənlis]	imóvel	and so on [ənd səu 'ɔn]	e assim por diante
quite a [kwait]	bastante	to ask one's way	perguntar o caminho
fantastic [fæn'tæstik]	fantástico, -a	to count [kaunt]	contar
anything like it ['eniθiŋ]	coisa semelhante	at least [ət 'liːst]	pelo menos
		Broadway ['brɔːdwei]	nome de rua
bird's-eye view ['bəːdzai vjuː]	aspecto geral	to form [fɔːm]	formar
		diagonal [dai'ægənl]	diagonal
wonderful ['wʌndəful]	maravilhoso	brilliant ['briljənt]	brilhante
		lit up [lit 'ʌp]	iluminado, -a
		Wall Street ['wɔːl striːt]	nome de rua
		small [smɔːl]	pequeno, -a
		commercial [kə'məːʃəl]	comercial

financial [fai'nænʃəl]	financeiro, -a
fence [fens]	vedação
to protect [prə'tekt]	proteger
enemy ['enimi]	inimigo
wild [waild]	selvagem
beast [biːst]	animal
wolf [wulf]	lobo
bear [bɛə]	urso
patch [pætʃ]	superfície
green [griːn]	verde
Central Park ['sentrəl 'pɑːk]	*parque de Nova Iorque*
lake ['leik]	lago
zoo [zuː]	jardim zoológico
elegant ['eligənt]	elegante
negro ['niːgrəu]	negro
Harlem ['hɑːləm]	*bairro de Nova Iorque*
Holland ['hɔlənd]	Holanda
Puerto Rican ['pwəːtəu 'riːkən]	porto-riquenho
safe [seif]	seguro, -a
to wander ['wɔndə]	passear
alone [ə'ləun]	só

30

conversation [kɔnvə'seiʃən]	conversa
drugstore ['drʌgstɔː]	«drugstore»
to surprise [sə'praiz]	surpreender
stool [stuːl]	banco
to display [dis'plei]	expor
cosmetic [kɔs'metik]	cosmético
confectionery [kən'fekʃnəri]	pastelaria
stationery [steiʃnəri]	papelaria
cigarette [sigə'ret]	cigarro
magazine [mægə'ziːn]	revista
household equipment ['haushəuld i'kwipmənt]	artigos de ménage
telephone booth *IA* ['telifəun 'buːð]	cabina telefónica
dispensary [dis'pensəri]	farmácia
to make up [meik], made, made [meid]	aviar
prescription [pri'skripʃən]	receita
order ['ɔːdə]	encomenda
hot dog ['hɔt 'dɔg]	cachorro
ice-cream ['ais'kriːm]	gelado
to continue [kən'tinju]	continuar
way of life ['wei əv 'laif]	modo de vida
American [ə'merikən]	americano, -a
maybe ['meibiː]	talvez
neither...nor ['naiðə...'nɔː]	nem...nem...
hedge [hedʒ]	sebe
to separate ['sepəreit]	separar
privacy ['privəsi]	privacidade
to exist [ig'zist]	existir
among [ə'mʌŋ]	entre
individual [indi'vidjuəl]	individual
sociable ['səuʃəbl]	sociável
exaggerate [ig'zædʒəreit]	exagerar
in need [niːd]	com necessidade
whenever [wen'evə]	sempre que
necessary ['nesisəri]	necessário
everybody ['evribɔdi]	toda a gente
to depend on [di'pend]	ter confiança em
spirit ['spirit]	espírito
pioneer [paiə'niə]	pioneiro
alive [ə'laiv]	vivo, -a
state [steit]	Estado
twentieth-century ['twentiiθ'sentʃuri]	século XX

Índice de matérias

Os números referem-se a páginas

about 59, 103
above 93
across 113
Adjectivo 32-35, 38, 40; graus com dupla forma 34, graus formados com -er, -est 33, graus irregulares 34, graus precedidos de more, most 33, particularidades do aspecto gráfico 33
Advérbio 38-41, 64-65; advérbios com dupla forma 40, advérbios derivados 39, advérbios interrogativos 29, advérbios simples 39, graus dos advérbios 40, lugar das expressões adverbiais na frase 64-65, «muito» 41, perífrase adverbial 39-40.
after 118-119
against 108
ago 135
along 153
among 88
around 103
Artigo 16, 129-130, 135; artigo definido 16, 129--130, artigo indefinido 16, 135
as far as 72
at 26, 130
be 17-18, 55, 58, 91
before 118
behind 118
below 99
beside(s) 158
between 87
beyond 108
but 158
by 131
can-could 58, 80
Comparação 35

Complemento directo acompanhado de infinito 111
Complemento indirecto: pronome pessoal 24, Condicional 85, 86
Conjunções 162
Conjuntivo 133-134, 137--139
Consoantes 12-13
dare 87
Datas 49
«deixar, mandar, fazer com que» 145-146
Determinantes possessivos 18
Dias da semana 50
Discurso directo 134
Discurso indirecto 134
Ditongos 11-12
do 91-92, enfático 88, 137
down 77
during 143
Emprego de to do 91-92
Emprego dos tempos 61-65
Estações do ano 50
except 158
for 143
from 71
Futuro 69-71, americano 161
Gerúndio 121-124
Graus dos adjectivos 32--34, dos advérbios 40
have 17-18, 55, 58, 91, 92
Horas 46
Imperativo 38, 92, 133
in 65
Indicações de valor 45
Infinito 17, 105-107
Inglês americano 151-153, 156-158, 161-162
inside 139
into 26, 66
may-might 58, 81

Meses 50
must 58, 82
near 131
need 87
Negativa 91-92
Numerais cardinais 43-45
Numerais ordinais 48-49
Números fraccionários 49
Números frequentativos 50
of 148
off 148-149
on 125
Ordem das palavras 64, 102, 125, 147-148
ought to 79, 85-86, 106
out of 66
outside 139
over 93
Particípio 53-54, 57-58, 115-117
Particularidades do aspecto gráfico (adjectivos) 33, do inglês americano 161, do particípio 74, do plural 21, 46, 51, dos verbos 20, 54, 74
Passagem de um estado para outro 145
Passiva 96-99, 101-102, 107
past 153
Past Participle 53-54, 57--58, 115-117
Past Perfect 61, 64
Past Tense 53-55, 57, 58
Plural 21, 46, 51, 55, 76--77
Preposições 26, 59, 65, 71, 77, 82-83, 87-88, 93, 99, 103, 108, 113, 118, 125, 130-131, 135, 139, 143, 148-149, 153, 158
Present Participle 74, 115-117

209

Present Perfect 61, 62-63
Present Tense 17-18 61, 62
Progressive Form 74-76, 142
Pronomes e Determinantes Demonstrativos 29-30
Pronomes Interrogativos 28
Pronomes Pessoais 16, 24
Pronomes Possessivos 18
Pronomes Reflexos 25
Pronomes Relativos 29--30, 124-125
Pronúncia 10-14, americana 156-158
round 103
shall-should 58, 85-86
since 135
Substantivo, caso possessivo 21-22, género 26, plural 21, 46, 51, 55, 76--77
Substituto «one» 58-59
Sujeito com infinito 112
that 29-30, 124-125
through 113
till 72
to 71
towards 108
until 72
up 77
used to 86, 106
Verbo, Forma enfática 93, 142, Tempos Compostos 61, 62-64, 69-71, 162
Verbos Auxiliares 17-18, 55
Verbos Defectivos 58, 79--82, 85-87
Verbos Intransitivos 97-98
Verbos Irregulares, 54, 66, 72, 77, 83, 88, 94, 99--100, 103, 108, 113, 119, 126, 131, 135, 140, 149, 153, 158, 162
Verbos Transitivos, 97-98
Vogais, 10-11
will-would 58, 86-87
with 26, 82
within 83
without 83